Mobile Forensics Cookbook

Data acquisition, extraction, recovery techniques, and investigations using modern forensic tools

Igor Mikhaylov

BIRMINGHAM - MUMBAI

Mobile Forensics Cookbook

Copyright © 2017 Packt Publishing

First published: December 2017

Production reference: 1141217

Published by Packt Publishing Ltd.
Livery Place
35 Livery Street
Birmingham
B3 2PB, UK.

ISBN 978-1-78528-205-8

www.packtpub.com

Credits

Author
Igor Mikhaylov

Copy Editor
Safis Editing

Reviewer
Rohit Tamma

Project Coordinator
Virginia Dias

Commissioning Editor
Kartikey Pandey

Proofreader
Safis Editing

Acquisition Editor
Rahul Nair

Indexer
Francy Puthiry

Content Development Editor
Sharon Raj

Graphics
Kirk D'Penha
Tania Dutta

Technical Editor
Mohit Hassija

Production Coordinator
Nilesh Mohite

About the Author

Igor Mikhaylov has been working as a forensics expert for 21 years. During this time, he had attended a lot of seminars and training classes in top forensic companies (such as Guidance Software, AccessData, and Cellebrite) and forensic departments of government organizations in the Russian Federation. He has experience and skills in computer forensics, incident response, cellphones forensics, chip-off forensics, malware forensics, data recovery, digital images analysis, video forensics, big data, and other fields. He has worked on several thousand forensic cases. When he works on a forensic case, he examines evidence using in-depth, industry-leading tools and techniques. He uses forensic software and hardware from leaders in the forensics industry. He has written three tutorials on cellphone forensics and incident response for Russian-speaking forensics experts.

He is the reviewer of *Windows Forensics Cookbook* by Oleg Skulkin and Scar de Courcier, Packt Publishing.

I would like to thank various people for their contribution to this book—All people from the Packt team for their valuable technical support; Vladimir Katalov (ElcomSoft Co.Ltd.), Oleg Fedorov (Oxygen Forensics, Inc.), Yury Gubanov (Belkasoft®), and Anton Evgraschenkov (Lan Project, a partner of Cellebrite) who shared their software for this book.

I'd like to thank my family—my wife Olga and our two sons, Max and Ilya. I really appreciate their patience and understanding.

I'd also like to thank Oleg Skulkin, Andrew Rubtsov, and Evgeniy Chapurin for their useful and constructive recommendations on this book; thank you, gentlemen.

About the Reviewer

Rohit Tamma is a Security Program Manager currently working with Microsoft. With over 8 years of experience in the field of security, his background spans management and technical consulting roles in the areas of application and cloud security, mobile security, penetration testing, and security training. His past experiences includes working with Accenture, ADP, and TCS, driving security programs for various client teams. Rohit has also coauthored a couple of books, such as *Practical Mobile Forensics* and *Learning Android Forensics* by Packt Publishing, which explain various techniques to perform forensics on mobile platforms. You can contact him on Twitter at @RohitTamma.

www.PacktPub.com

For support files and downloads related to your book, please visit `www.PacktPub.com`. Did you know that Packt offers eBook versions of every book published, with PDF and ePub files available? You can upgrade to the eBook version at `www.PacktPub.com` and as a print book customer, you are entitled to a discount on the eBook copy. Get in touch with us at `service@packtpub.com` for more details.

At `www.PacktPub.com`, you can also read a collection of free technical articles, sign up for a range of free newsletters and receive exclusive discounts and offers on Packt books and eBooks.

`https://www.packtpub.com/mapt`

Get the most in-demand software skills with Mapt. Mapt gives you full access to all Packt books and video courses, as well as industry-leading tools to help you plan your personal development and advance your career.

Why subscribe?

- Fully searchable across every book published by Packt
- Copy and paste, print, and bookmark content
- On demand and accessible via a web browser

Customer Feedback

Thanks for purchasing this Packt book. At Packt, quality is at the heart of our editorial process. To help us improve, please leave us an honest review on this book's Amazon page at

Thanks for purchasing this Packt book. At Packt, quality is at the heart of our editorial process. To help us improve, please leave us an honest review on this book's Amazon page at `https://www.amazon.com/dp/1785282050`.

If you'd like to join our team of regular reviewers, you can email us at `customerreviews@packtpub.com`. We award our regular reviewers with free eBooks and videos in exchange for their valuable feedback. Help us be relentless in improving our products!

If you'd like to join our team of regular reviewers, you can email us at `customerreviews@packtpub.com`. We award our regular reviewers with free eBooks and videos in exchange for their valuable feedback. Help us be relentless in improving our products!

Table of Contents

Preface

Mobile devices (such as phones, smartphones, tablets, and other electronic gadgets) are everywhere in our life. We use them every day. Users are increasingly using mobile devices as a means of communicating with other people. It's not just voice calls. This is communication through various instant messaging (such as Skype, iChat, WhatsApp, and Viber) and social networking applications (such as Facebook).

Usually, mobile devices contain a lot of personal data about their owners.

In this book, we will deal with forensic tools for mobile forensics and practical tips and tricks for successfully using them.

What this book covers

Chapter 1, *SIM Card Acquisition and Analysis*, will guide you through SIM card acquisition and analysis with TULP2G, MOBILedit Forensic, Oxygen Forensic, and Simcon. You will also learn how to analyze SIM cards with TULP2G, MOBILedit Forensic, Oxygen Forensic, and Simcon.

Chapter 2, *Android Device Acquisition*, will teach you how to acquire data from Android devices with Oxygen Forensic, MOBILedit Forensic, Belkasoft Acquisition Tool, Magnet Acquire, and Smart Switch.

Chapter 3, *Apple Device Acquisition*, will teach you the acquisition of different iOS devices. You will learn how to acquire data from iOS devices with Oxygen Forensic, libmobiledevice, Elcomsoft iOS Toolkit, and iTunes.

Chapter 4, *Windows Phone and BlackBerry Acquisition*, will explain the acquisition of different Windows Phone devices and BlackBerry devices. You will also learn how to acquire data from Windows Phone devices and BlackBerry devices with Oxygen Forensic, BlackBerry Desktop Software, and UFED 4PC.

Chapter 5, *Clouds are Alternative Data Sources*, will deal with the acquisition of Clouds. In this chapter, you will also learn how to acquire data from Clouds with Cloud Extractor, Electronic Evidence Examiner, Elcomsoft Phone Breaker, and Belkasoft Evidence Center.

Chapter 6, *SQLite Forensics*, will teach you how to analyze SQLite databases. Also, you will learn how to extract and analyze data from SQLite databases with Belkasoft Evidence Center, DB Browser for SQLite, Oxygen Forensic SQLite Viewer, and SQLite Wizard.

Chapter 7, *Understanding Plist Forensics*, will help you to analyze plist files. You will learn how to extract and analyze data from plist files with Apple Plist Viewer, Belkasoft Evidence Center, plist Editor Pro, and Plist Explorer.

Chapter 8, *Analyzing Physical Dumps and Backups of Android Devices*, will teach you how to analyze data (physical dumps, backups, and so on) from Android devices. Also, you will learn how to extract and analyze the data with Autopsy, Oxygen Forensic, Belkasoft Evidence Center, Magnet AXIOM, and Encase Forensic.

Chapter 9, *iOS Forensics*, will explain how to analyze data from iOS devices. You will learn how to extract and analyze the data with iPhone Backup Extractor, UFED Physical Analyzer, BlackLight, Oxygen Forensic, Belkasoft Evidence Center, Magnet AXIOM, Encase Forensic, and Elcomsoft Phone Viewer.

Chapter 10, *Windows Phone and BlackBerry Forensics*, will teach how to analyze data from Windows Phone devices and BlackBerry devices. You will learn how to extract and analyze the data with Elcomsoft Blackberry Backup Explorer Pro, Oxygen Forensic, and UFED Physical Analyzer.

Chapter 11, *JTAG and Chip-off Techniques*, will show you how to extract data from locked or damaged Android devices, Windows Phone devices, and Apple devices.

What you need for this book

The following software is required for this book:

- AccessData FTK Imager
- Autopsy
- Belkasoft Acquisition
- Belkasoft Evidence Center
- BlackBerry Desktop Software
- BlackLigh
- Cellebrite UFED4PC
- DB Browser for SQLite
- Elcomsoft Blackberry Backup Explorer Pro
- Elcomsoft iOS Toolkit

- Elcomsoft Phone Breaker
- Elcomsoft Phone Viewer
- Encase Forensic
- iPhone Backup Extractor
- iThmb Converter
- iTunes
- libmobiledevice
- Magnet AXIOM
- Magnet Acquire
- MobilEdit Forensics
- Oxygen Software
- Paraben Electronic Evidence Examiner
- PC 3000 Flash
- Plist Editor Pro
- Plist Explorer
- SIMCon
- Smart Switch
- ThumbExpert
- TULP2G
- UFED Physical Analyzer
- Z3X EasyJtag BOX JTAG Classic Suite

Most of the commercial tools in this list have trial versions available that can be downloaded for free. Download links are provided in the chapters.

Who this book is for

If you are a mobile forensic analyst, forensic analyst, or digital forensic student who wants to conduct mobile forensic investigations on different platforms, such as Android OS, iOS, Windows Phone, or BlackBerry OS, then this book is for you.

Sections

In this book, you will find several headings that appear frequently (*Getting ready*, *How to do it...*, *How it works...*, *There's more...*, and *See also*). To give clear instructions on how to complete a recipe, we use these sections as follows:

Getting ready

This section tells you what to expect in the recipe, and describes how to set up any software or any preliminary settings required for the recipe.

How to do it...

This section contains the steps required to follow the recipe.

How it works...

This section usually consists of a detailed explanation of what happened in the previous section.

There's more...

This section consists of additional information about the recipe in order to make the reader more knowledgeable about the recipe.

See also

This section provides helpful links to other useful information for the recipe.

Conventions

In this book, you will find a number of text styles that distinguish between different kinds of information. Here are some examples of these styles and an explanation of their meaning. Code words in text, database table names, folder names, filenames, file extensions, pathnames, dummy URLs, user input, and Twitter handles are shown as follows: "On the TULP2G download page (`https://sourceforge.net/projects/tulp2g/files/`), select the `TULP2G-installer-1.4.0.4.msi` file and download it."

A block of code is set as follows:

```
;Google Nexus One
%SingleAdbInterface%        = USB_Install, USB\VID_18D1&PID_0D02
%CompositeAdbInterface%     = USB_Install, USB\VID_18D1&PID_0D02&MI_01
%SingleAdbInterface%        = USB_Install, USB\VID_18D1&PID_4E11
%CompositeAdbInterface%     = USB_Install, USB\VID_18D1&PID_4E12&MI_01
```

New terms and **important words** are shown in bold. Words that you see on the screen, for example, in menus or dialog boxes, appear in the text like this: "When the program is launched, click on the **Open Profile...** button."

Warnings or important notes appear like this.

Tips and tricks appear like this.

Reader feedback

Feedback from our readers is always welcome. Let us know what you think about this book-what you liked or disliked. Reader feedback is important for us as it helps us develop titles that you will really get the most out of. To send us general feedback, simply email feedback@packtpub.com, and mention the book's title in the subject of your message. If there is a topic that you have expertise in and you are interested in either writing or contributing to a book, see our author guide at www.packtpub.com/authors.

Customer support

Now that you are the proud owner of a Packt book, we have a number of things to help you to get the most from your purchase.

Errata

Although we have taken every care to ensure the accuracy of our content, mistakes do happen. If you find a mistake in one of our books-maybe a mistake in the text or the code-we would be grateful if you could report this to us. By doing so, you can save other readers from frustration and help us improve subsequent versions of this book. If you find any errata, please report them by visiting http://www.packtpub.com/submit-errata, selecting your book, clicking on the **Errata Submission Form** link, and entering the details of your errata. Once your errata are verified, your submission will be accepted and the errata will be uploaded to our website or added to any list of existing errata under the Errata section of that title. To view the previously submitted errata, go to https://www.packtpub.com/books/content/support and enter the name of the book in the search field. The required information will appear in the **Errata** section.

Piracy

Piracy of copyrighted material on the internet is an ongoing problem across all media. At Packt, we take the protection of our copyright and licenses very seriously. If you come across any illegal copies of our works in any form on the internet, please provide us with the location address or website name immediately so that we can pursue a remedy. Please contact us at copyright@packtpub.com with a link to the suspected pirated material. We appreciate your help in protecting our authors and our ability to bring you valuable content.

Questions

If you have a problem with any aspect of this book, you can contact us at questions@packtpub.com, and we will do our best to address the problem.

1
SIM Card Acquisition and Analysis

In this chapter, we'll cover the following recipes:

- SIM card acquisition and analysis with TULP2G
- SIM card acquisition and analysis with MOBILedit Forensics
- SIM card acquisition and analysis with SIMCon
- SIM card acquisition and analysis with Oxygen Forensic

Introduction

The main function of a SIM card is the identification of a user of a cellular phone on the network so that they can get access to its services.

The following types of data, which are valuable for an expert or investigator, can be found in the SIM card:

- Information related to the services provided by the mobile operator
- Phonebook and information about calls
- Information about messages exchanged
- Location information

Initially, SIM cards were almost the only source of data about the contacts of the mobile device owner, as the information about the phonebook, calls, and messages could be found only in their memory. Later, the storage of these data was relocated to the mobile devices memory and SIM cards began to be used only to identify subscribers in cellular networks. This is why some of the forensic tools developers, for the examination of mobile devices, decided not to include the SIM cards examination function in their products. However, today there are a lot of cheap phones (often, we call them "Chinese phones") with limited memory capacity. In these phones, part of the phone owners' data is stored in the SIM cards. This is why the forensic examination of SIM cards remains relevant.

SIM card is a regular smart card. It contains the following main components:

- Processor
- RAM
- ROM
- EEPROM
- A file system
- Controller I/O

In practice, we come across two kinds of SIM cards with six and eight contacts on the contact pads. This happens because the two contacts do not directly interact with the phone (smartphone) and their absence decreases the size of the area occupied by a SIM card when it is placed in the mobile device.

SIM cards can use three types of supply voltage (VCC): 5 V, 3.3 V, 1.8 V. Each card has a particular supply voltage.

There is an overvoltage protection in SIM cards. This is why when a 3.3 V supply voltage SIM card is placed in the card reader, that can operate only with 5 V supply voltage (old models), neither the information nor the SIM card can be damaged, and it will be impossible to work with this SIM card. As such, an expert may think that the SIM card is faulty. However, it is not so.

The forensic examination of a SIM card, before data extraction from the mobile device, where it is installed, is unreasonable. As the user's data stored in the memory of the mobile device, it can be reset or deleted during the process of removing the SIM card.

For analysis, a SIM card has to be removed from the mobile device and connected to the expert's computer via a specific device: a card reader.

Based on the previously mentioned information about SIM cards, we can figure out the main requirements to a card reader device with which it will be comfortable for an expert to examine SIM cards:

- The card reader device has to support smart cards with supply voltage of 5 V, 3.3 V, and 1.8 V.
- The card reader device has to support smart cards with six and eight contacts on the contact pads.
- The card reader device has to support Microsoft PC/SC protocol. Drivers for this kind of devices are pre-installed on all versions of the Windows operating systems. This is why there is no need to install additional drivers in order to connect such devices to the expert's computer.

The following image shows an example of such a card reader:

SIM cards reader produced by «ASR» company, model «ACR38T».

Despite the fact that there are card reader devices designed for reading data from SIM cards, card reader devices designed for reading data from the standard size cards (having the size of a bank card) can be used. To work comfortably with these devices, a blank card, to which the SIM card is adjusted with some small pieces of tape, is used.

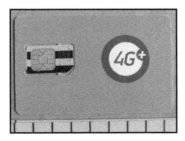

This is a SIM card adjusted with a bank card looks.

SIM card acquisition and analysis with TULP2G

TULP2G is a free tool developed by Netherlands Forensic Institute for forensic examination of SIM cards and cellular phones. Unfortunately, this program has not been updated for a long time. However, it can be used for very old cellular phones and SIM cards data acquisition and analysis.

Getting ready

On the TULP2G download page (`https://sourceforge.net/projects/tulp2g/files/`), select the `TULP2G-installer-1.4.0.4.msi` file and download it. At the time of writing this, the most up-to-date version is 1.4.0.4. When the download is finished, double-click on this file. The installation process of the program will be started.

If the installation of the TULP2G program is performed in the Windows XP operating system, you need to install Microsoft Net Framework 2.0 and Windows Installer 3.1 before the installation of the TULP2G. The programs mentioned previously can be downloaded from the Microsoft Corporation website.

How to do it...

1. When the program is launched, click on the **Open Profile...** button:

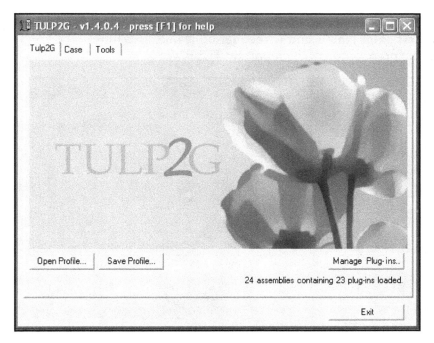

The main window of the TULP2G program

2. In the opened window, you will find profiles, one of which has to be loaded in the program. Select the **TULP2G.Profile.SIM-Investigation** profile, and then click on **Open**.

Data extraction profiles of TULP2G

3. In the **Case/Investigation Settings** window, fill in the fields: **Case Name**, **Investigator Name**, and **Investigation Name**. This information will be used later in the preparation of the report by TULP2G.

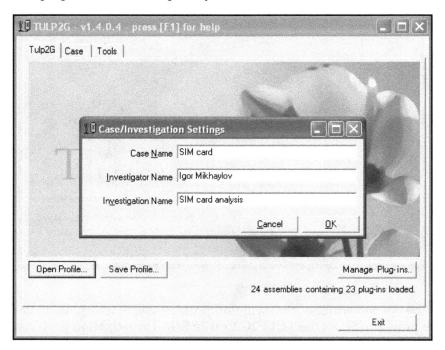

The Case/Investigation Settings window

4. In the next window, **TULP2G - SIM card;** for the **Communication Plug-in** field, set the value as PC/SC chip card communication [1.4.0.3]. For the **Protocol Plug-in** field, set the value as SIM/USIM chip card data extraction [1.4.0.7]. If the examined SIM card has PIN or PUK code, enter it by clicking on the **Configure** button, which is located next to the **Protocol Plug-in** field.

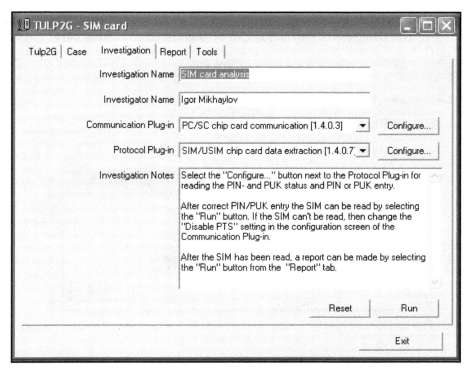

Window TULP2G - SIM card.

Reading data from the examined SIM card will not be possible if the PIN or PUK code are not entered.

5. Click on the **Run** button. The process of data extraction from the SIM card will begin. The progress of extraction can be seen in the progress bar.

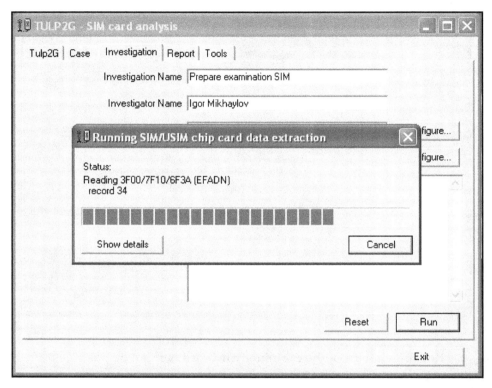

The progress bar.

6. When the data is extracted from the SIM card, you can conduct a new extraction or generate a report about the extraction that has been performed. To generate the report, go to the **Report** tab. In the **Report Name** field, enter the name of the report; in the **Export Plug-in** and **Selected Conversion Plug-in(s)** fields, select plugins that will be used for the report generation. In the **Selected Investigation(s)** field, select those extractions for which you want to generate the report, and then click on **Run**.

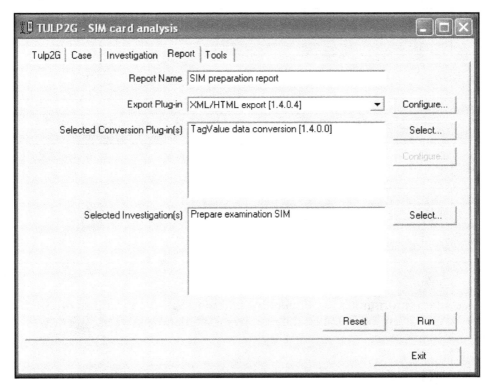

The options window for the report generation

7. When the report generation process is finished, there will be two files with formats HTML and XML. The HTML file can be opened with any web browser.

Netherlands Forensic Institute - TULP2G

Case name	SIM card analysis
Case creator	Igor Mikhaylov
Creation date	11.04.2017 11:14:17
MD5 hash	F202E4EAC3F10C9140F660F9FBFD36D8
SHA-1 hash	6BC239335A65D397AC7A2C89B3A4DC48F2C69A3C

Plug-in info

Plug-in type	Plug-in info
ExportPlugin	TULP2G.Export.XML, Version=1.4.0.4, Culture=neutral, PublicKeyToken=3480a3624ac48f93
ConversionPlugin	TULP2G.Conversion.TagValue, Version=1.4.0.0, Culture=neutral, PublicKeyToken=3480a3624ac48f93

Investigation *Prepare examination SIM*

Investigator	Igor Mikhaylov
Creation date	11.04.2017 11:14:17
MD5 hash	5E3DD2287DAC0A7AFB0890AB7B7982B3
SHA-1 hash	FA401AE4E9B2756696BB48BBB8A068242DEEB9EC

A fragment of the report

These files contain information (a phonebook, text messages, calls, and so on) that was extracted from the examined SIM card. It can be viewed and analyzed.

How it works...

TULP2G extracts data from the SIM card that is installed in the card reader, which is connected to the expert's computer, and generates a report. During the verification process, MD5 and SHA1 hashes of the image and the source are being compared.

See also

- The TULP2G project website: `http://tulp2g.sourceforge.net`
- The TULP2G download page: `https://sourceforge.net/projects/tulp2g/files/`

SIM card acquisition and analysis with MOBILedit Forensics

MOBILedit Forensic is a commercial forensic software by the company Compelson. It is updated regularly. This program can extract data from phones, smartphones, and SIM cards. As the program developers state, MOBILedit Forensic is a program that allows us to extract data from a phone or SIM card with a minimum number of steps. Also, this program has a unique function on which we will focus in another chapter.

Getting ready

On the MOBILedit download page (`http://www.mobiledit.com/download-list/mobiledit-forensic`), click on DOWNLOAD. When the downloading process is finished, double-click on the downloaded file of the program and install it. After the first run of the program, you need to enter the license key. If the license key is not entered, the program will work in the trial mode for 7 days.

How to do it...

There are two ways of extracting data from SIM cards with MOBILedit Forensic:

1. Extracting data through wizard
2. Extracting data through the main window of the MOBILedit Forensic program

In this book, we will focus on the data extraction from SIM card via the main window of the MOBILedit Forensic program.

When you run the program, the information about the connected card reader will appear in the upper left corner of the main window of the MOBILedit Forensic program.

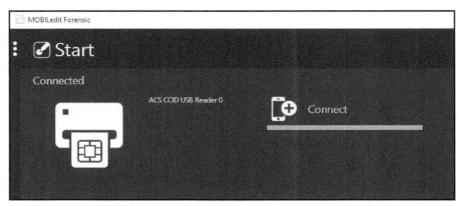

A fragment of the main window

If you click on **Connect**, the MOBILedit Forensic Wizard will start, through which you can extract data from mobile devices and SIM cards.
Let's now see how to extract the data:

1. Click on the image of the card reader. The information about **Answer on Reset(ART) and ICCID** of the SIM card will be displayed. If this SIM card is locked, you will be asked to enter the PIN or PUK code.

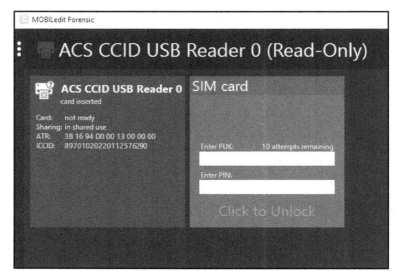

Fragment of the main window with information about the SIM card

2. After entering the PIN or PUK codes, the SIM card will be unlocked and the **Report Wizard** option will appear on the main window. The fact that the examined SIM card was unlocked is indicated by the displayed **International Code (IMSI)**, access to which is possible only after entering the correct PIN code.

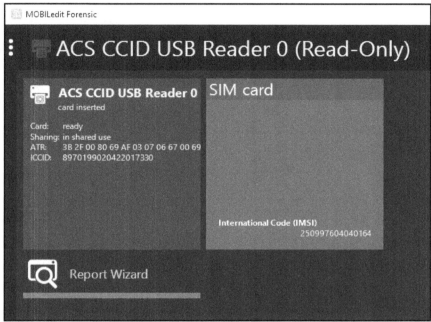

A fragment of the main window with information about the SIM card

3. Click on the **Report Wizard**; it will open the **MOBILedit Forensic Wizard** window, which will extract data from the SIM card and generate a report.

4. Fill in the fields **Device Label, Device Name, Device Evidence Number, Owner Phone Number, Owner Name,** and **Phone Notes** . Then click on the **Next** button.

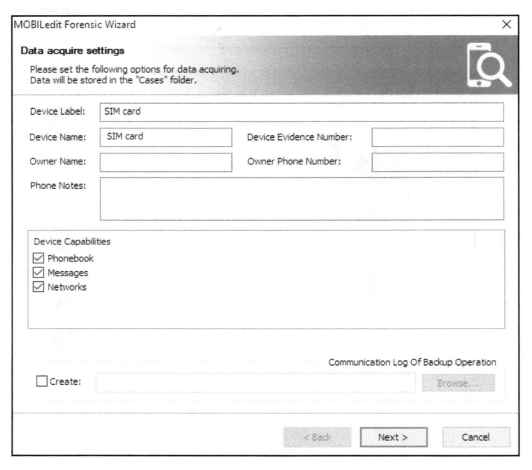

Window MOBILedit Forensic Wizard

5. The data will be extracted. The extraction status will be displayed in the **MOBILedit Forensic Wizard** window.

6. When the extraction is finished, click on the **Next** button. After that, `MOBILedit Forensic Wizard` will display the following window:

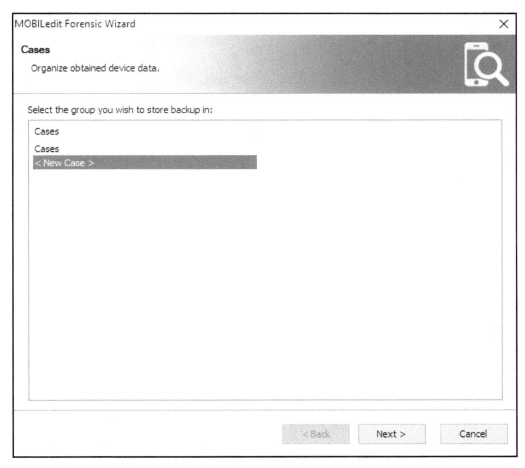

The MOBILedit Forensic Wizard window

7. Click on **New Case**. In the opened window, fill in the **Label**, **Number**, **Name**, **E-mail**, **Phone Number**, and **Notes** fields, and then click on the **Next** button.

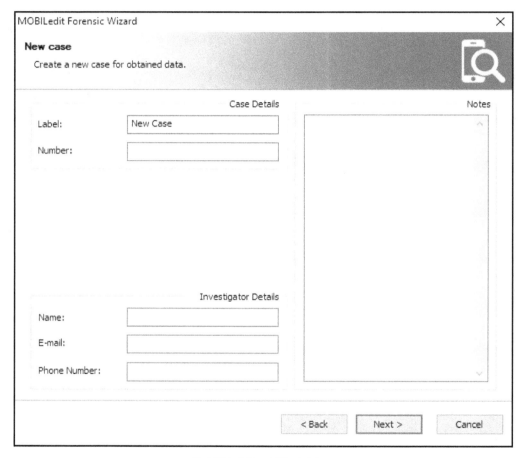

The MOBILedit Forensic Wizard window

8. In the next window of **MOBILedit Forensic Wizard**, select the format in which the report will be generated and click on the **Finish** button.

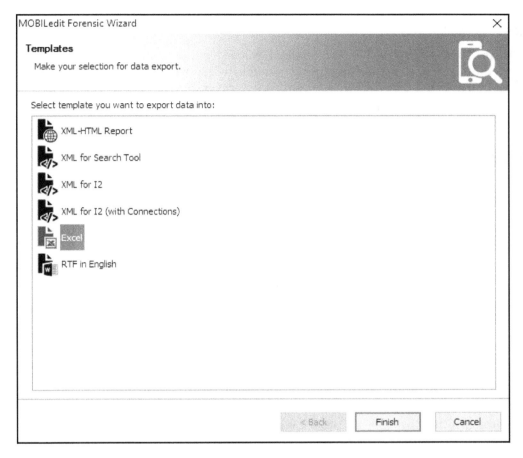

Final window of MOBILedit Forensic Wizard

A forensic report about the extraction will be generated in the selected format.

How it works...

MOBILedit Forensics extracts data from the SIM card installed in the card reader that is connected to the expert's computer and generates the report, taking the minimum number of steps. It is useful if there are a lot of mobile devices or SIM cards that have to be investigated, as it speeds up the process of data extraction.

See also

- The MOBILedit Forensics website at http://www.mobiledit.com.
- The MOBILedit Forensics download page at http://www.mobiledit.com/download-list/mobiledit-forensic.

SIM card acquisition and analysis with SIMCon

SIMCon is one of the best utilities for a forensic analysis of SIM cards. It had a low price and for government organizations, military, and police, it was provided free of charge. Besides its impressive functionality, SIMCon, from some SIM cards, can extract data protected by PIN code. For example, phonebook.

Despite the fact that the SIMCon project was closed several years ago, the program did not disappear. A new updated version of this program is called **Sim Card Seizure**. The distribution rights of the program belong to the company Paraben. Also, the functionality of SIMCon is implemented in another product from Paraben--E3: Electronic Evidence Examiner.

Getting ready

The SIMCon project does not have its own address on the internet now. However, the installation software can be found via search engines.You can also download a trial version of Sim Card Seizure from Paraben's website. The limitation of the trial version of Sim Card Seizure is that only the first 20 records of phonebook, calls, messages are displayed.

How to do it...

1. Double-click on the program icon and connect the card reader with the SIM card. The program will open the **Enter PIN** information window as shown in the following screenshot:

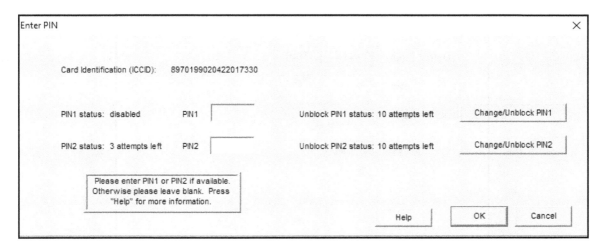

2. In this case, there is no need to enter the PIN code. Click on the **OK** button to start the data extraction process. The status of the extraction process will be shown in the **Reading SIM...** window:

3. If the data is successfully extracted, you will be asked to fill in the **Investigator:**, **Date / Time:**, **Case:**, **Evidence Number:**, and **Notes:** fields in the **Acquisition Notes** window. After filling in the fields, click on the **OK** button:

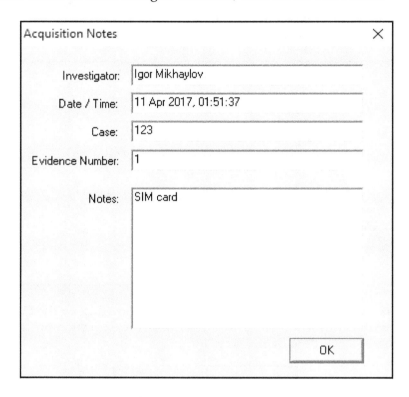

4. Unlike TULP2G and MOBILedit Forensic, SIMCon allows you not only to extract data and generate a report but also to view the extracted data. The following screenshot shows a fragment of the SIMCon window in which we can see SMS messages, including deleted ones, which were extracted from the SIM card:

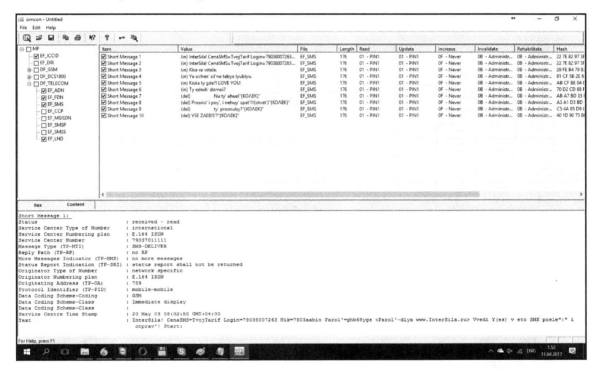

The Acquisition Notes window

At the bottom of the SIMCon main window, there is a section that displays detailed information about the selected record:

```
Hex          Content

Short Message 1:
Status                                  : received - read
Service Center Type of Number           : international
Service Center Numbering plan           : E.164 ISDN
Service Center Number                    : 79037011111
Message Type (TP-MTI)                    : SMS-DELIVER
Reply Path (TP-RP)                       : no RP
More Messages Indicator (TP-MMS)         : no more messages
Status Report Indication (TP-SRI)        : status report shall not be returned
Originator Type of Number                : network specific
Originator Numbering plan                : E.164 ISDN
Originating Address (TP-OA)              : 789
Protocol Identifier (TP-PID)            : mobile-mobile
Data Coding Scheme-Coding                : GSM
Data Coding Scheme-Class                 : Immediate display
Data Coding Scheme-Class                 :
Service Centre Time Stamp                : 20 May 03 08:02:50 GMT+04:00
Text                                     : InterSila! CenaSMS=TvojTarif Login=790
                                           otprav'! Start:
```

A section of the SIMCon main window with the detailed information about the selected record

The SIMCon program allows viewing the contents of each file. The following screenshot shows the contents of the elementary file (EF_ICCID):

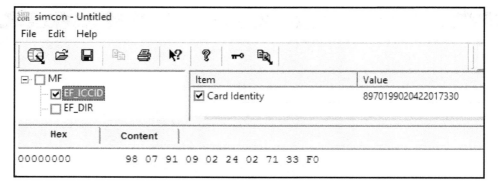

How it works...

SIMCon extracts data from the SIM card installed in the card reader that is connected to the expert's computer. After this, you can generate a forensic report or analyze the extracted data from the main window of this program.

See also

- The Sim Card Seizure program's website: `https://www.paraben-sticks.com/sim-card-seizure.html`
- The E3: Electronic Evidence Examiner program's website: `https://www.paraben.com/products/e3-universal`

SIM card acquisition and analysis with Oxygen Forensic

Oxygen Forensic is one of the best programs for mobile forensics. This program has a function of SIM card analysis besides its other functions. The program is commercial, but there is a 30-day trial full version, which you can get on request. When the request is accepted, you will receive an email in which you will find a registry key and instructions for downloading the installation software.

Getting ready

Download the Oxygen Forensic (`https://www.oxygen-forensic.com/en/`). Install it with the help of prompts. Go through the menu path: **Service|Enter Key**. In the opened License window, enter the license key and click on the **Save** button. Restart the program.

How to do it...

In order to examine a SIM card, you need to remove it from a mobile device and then install it in the SIM card reader, which has to be connected to the expert's computer. As we mentioned earlier, Microsoft PC/SC drivers are pre-installed on the Windows operating systems meaning that there is no need to install anything else.

Now let's see how to use Oxygen Forensic:

1. In the Oxygen Forensic program, click on the **Connect** device button that is located in the toolbar. It will start **Oxygen Forensic Extractor**:

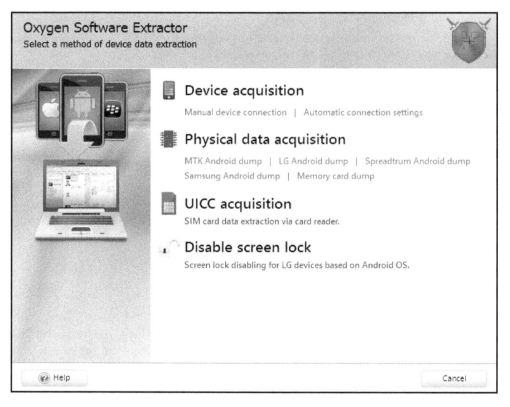

The main window of Oxygen Forensic Extractor

2. In the main menu of **Oxygen Forensic Extractor,** click on the **UICC acquisition** option. The next window will prompt you to select the connected card reader or it will display an error message:

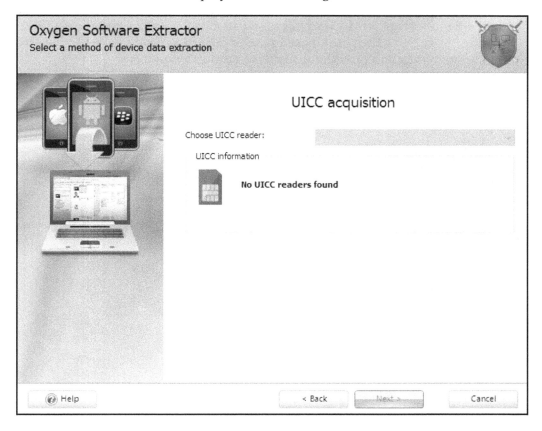

A card reader connection error message

3. If access to a SIM card data is limited by a PIN or PUK code, you will be prompted to enter the appropriate code. The number of available attempts to enter PIN and PUK codes is displayed in the program. If there were no attempts to unlock the SIM card, then there should be 3 attempts to enter the PIN code and 10 attempts to enter the PUK code. After 10 failed attempts to enter the PUK code, the SIM card will be blocked forever. The PUK code can be received from the communication provider through an authorized person.

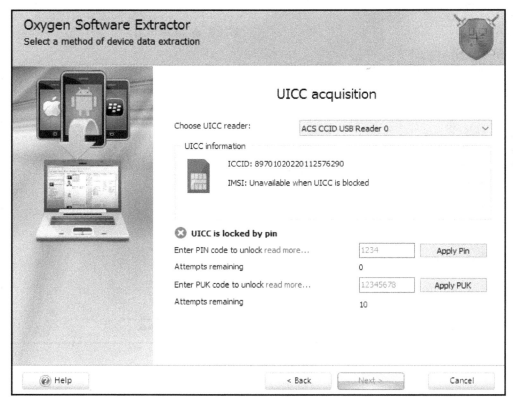

The SIM card data extraction window

The SIM card data extraction window displays the following:

- Information about the card reader
- Information about the SIM card
- Fields for entering PIN and PUK codes

Enter the SIM card unlock code and click on the **Next** button.

4. In the next window, you can specify additional information about the extraction that will be stored in the case. Also, in this window, you can select the options to save the extracted data from the device:

The **Stored extracted physical dump of backup in the device image...** option saves the main files from the SIM card.

The **Complete UICC image** option saves all files from the SIM card. The SIM card files' extraction process may take over 12 hours if you select this option.

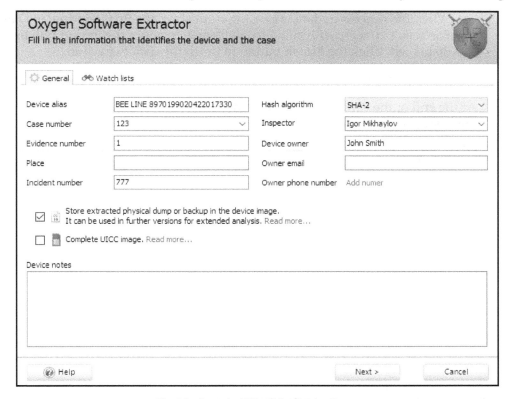

The window for entering additional information about the case

5. Click on the **Next** button. The process of extracting data from the investigated SIM card will start.

The following data can be extracted from the SIM card, including the deleted ones:

- General information about the SIM card
- Contacts
- Calls
- Messages
- Other information

When the process of data importing is finished, the final window of Oxygen Forensic Extractor with summary information about the import will be displayed. Click the **Finish** button to finish the data extraction.

The extracted data will be available for viewing and analysis.

6. At the end of the extraction, the created case can be opened in the **Oxygen Forensic** program.

Summarized information about the extraction

7. Now click on **Messages** category. An appropriate section with the extracted data can be viewed in respect of the case.

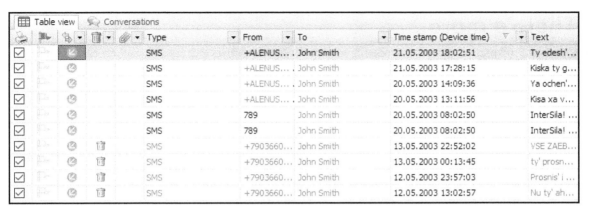

Viewing Messages section

8. Return on the main screen of Oxygen Forensic. Click on **File browser** category. In the **File browser** section, files that were extracted from the SIM card can be viewed. The analysis of these files contents can be done manually.

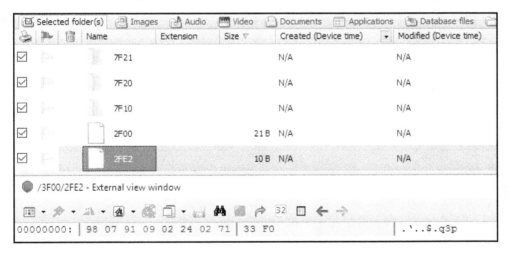

Viewing 2FE2 file contents

How it works...

Oxygen Forensic extracts data from the SIM card installed in the card reader that is connected to the expert's computer. After this, you can generate a forensic report or analyze the extracted data from the main window of this program.

There's more...

Oxygen Forensic displays the names of files in hex and this can be inconvenient for an expert. The following table shows the correspondence between the standard files' names in hex view and their content:

File name	Description	File name	Description
3F00	MF	6F05	EF (LP)
7F10	DF (TELECOM)	6F31	EF (HPLMN)
7F20	DF (GSM)	6F41	EF (PUCT)
7F21	DF (DCS1800)	6F78	EF (ACC)
2FE2	EF (ICCID)	6FAE	EF (PHASE)
6F3A	EF (AND)	6F07	EF (IMSI)
6F3C	EF (SMS)	6F37	EF (ACMmax)
6F40	EF (MSISDN)	6F45	EF (CBM)
6F43	EF (SMSS)	6F7B	EF (FPLMN)
6F4A	EF (EXT1)	6F52	EF (KcGPRS)
6F3B	EF (FDN)	6F20	EF (Kc)
6F3D	EF (CCP)	6F38	EF (SST)
6F42	EF (SIMSP)	6F46	EF (SPN)
6F44	EF (LND)	6F7E	EF (LOCI)
6F4B	EF (EXT2)	6F53	EF(LOCIGPRS)
6F74	EF (BCCH)	6F30	EF (PLMNcel)
6FAD	EF (AD)	6F54	EF (SUME)

See also

- The Oxygen Forensic program's website at https://www.oxygen-forensic.com/en/.

Android Device Acquisition

2

In this chapter, we'll cover the following recipes:

- Preparatory work
- Android device acquisition with Oxygen Forensic
- Android device acquisition with MOBILedit Forensic
- Android device acquisition with Belkasoft Evidence Center
- Android device acquisition with Magnet Acquire
- Making physical dumps of Android device without rooting
- Unlocking locked Android device
- Acquiring Android device through Wi-Fi
- Samsung Android device acquisition with Smart Switch

Introduction

Mobile devices running the Android operating system occupy more than 80% of the mobile devices market. The variety of the operating system versions and the hardware platforms on which they are used provide a wide range of data extraction methods. There is no such range of data extraction methods for any group of the following mobile devices: iOS devices, Windows Phone devices, and BlackBerry devices.

The most common methods of data extraction from Android devices are as follows:

- **Logical extraction**: This method allows to extract only certain types of logical data, such as Phonebook, Calls, Messages (SMS/MMS), and so on. As a rule, logical extraction requires the installation of an agent program that helps the mobile forensic software to extract data from a device. The installation of the program on the device is required by the hardware features of the memory structure and security policy of mobile devices.

- **Backup**: This method allows to extract only logical data from a device, such as Phonebook, Calls, Messages (SMS/MMS), video files, images, audio files, and so on. The information from applications (for example, from IM messengers) is transferred fully or partially into the created backup. It (whether the application data will be transferred or not) depends on the version of the operating system and the security settings of a mobile device. Often, there are situations where only the account information is transferred to the created backup from the installed application and it makes an expert think that the forensic software he uses does not support data extraction from this application, but if the expert extracts the file system or physical dump of the device instead of creating the backup, his forensic software will extract the application data (for example, chats).

- **File system extraction**: This method implies file system extraction from a device. All the files that are in the user's partition (as a rule, this partition is called userdata) are extracted when you use this method.

- **Physical dump**: This method implies creating the full copy of a device memory, which contains all the partitions of the device, including service data, applications, and user's data. Deleted files can be restored from the physical dump.

- **Joint Test Action Group (JTAG)**: We will focus on this method in `Chapter 11`, *JTAG and Chip-off Techniques*. JTAG – this method is named after the name of industry standard. JTAG is a standard used for testing system boards.

- **Chip-off**: We will focus on this method in `Chapter 11`, *JTAG and Chip-off Techniques*. Chip-off is a destructive method, which is based on the removing of memory chip from system board.

Despite the fact that Backup and file system extraction methods allow us to extract only logical data and files, it is possible for an expert to restore deleted records from SQLite data bases (such as Phonebook records, Calls, SMS messages, and mobile applications' data bases records).

In this chapter, we will cover the main methods of data extraction from the Android devices.

Preparatory work

You will have to perform a number of preparatory steps before performing data extraction from Android devices.

Preparing the mobile device

Before connecting the device to the computer, you need to activate the **USB Debugging** mode on the device. This mode enables the ADB server on the device.

USB Debugging is activated in the following ways:

For Android 2.0-2.3.x:

1. Go to the menu of the device.
2. Select **Settings.**
3. In the **Settings** section, select **Applications**.
4. In the **Applications** section, select **Development.**
5. In the **Development** section, select **USB Debugging**.

For Android 3.0 to 4.1.x :

1. Go to the menu of the device.
2. Select **Settings**.
3. In the **Settings** section, select **Developer Options**.
4. In the **Developer Options** section, select **USB Debugging**.
5. Click on **Ok** to confirm the activation of USB Debugging mode.

For Android 4.2.x and higher:

1. Go to the menu of the device.
2. Select **Settings**.
3. In the **Settings** section, select **About device**.
4. In the **About** phone section, tap the **Build Number** field seven times. Then, you will see this message: You are now a developer!

5. Go back to **Settings**.
6. Select **Developer Options**.
7. In the **Developer Options**, section select **USB Debugging.**

For Android 5.0 and higher:

1. Go to the menu of the device;
2. Select **Settings**.
3. In the **Settings** section, select **About device.**
4. In the **About** phone section, tap the **Build Number** field seven times Build Number. Then, you will see this message: You are now a developer!
5. Tap **Back** to go back to **Settings**.
6. Select **Developer Options**.
7. In the **Developer Options** section, select **USB Debugging.**
8. Click on **OK** to confirm the activation of USB Debugging mode.

When you connect the device to the computer, you must also select the correct USB mode in the device: **None**, **Charge only**, **MTP**, **PTP**, and so on. Each producer calls this mode in their own way. Never connect devices in the **Media mode**. If the Android device is Media mode, you are not able to create an Android backup of the device.

For successful connection of the device, you need to make sure that there is a memory card in the device, which should have at least 1 MB available space. During the logical extraction, the agent program uses the memory card for temporary files' storage, which are deleted when the reading is finished. Files that were stored in the memory card before connection are not changed or deleted. However, it is recommended that you use your own memory card and not the one that was in the examined device.

Preparing the workstation

In forensics, one of the important steps is to make sure that the evidence is not tampered with and if for some reason changes are to be made to the evidence. Example - unlocking, the changes are to be documented carefully. Other precautionary measures such as using sterile and dedicated forensic workstation should also be highlighted.

You have to install the drivers of the Android device before you connect it to the workstation. The device's drivers can be found in the internet. When the drivers are installed you should reboot the computer.

Before you connect the device to the computer for the first time, unlock the device (if it is locked) and connect it. You will see the **Allow USB Debugging** request on the screen of the device. Tick the field **Always allow from this computer** and tap **Allow**.

You need to make sure that the drivers were installed correctly. On your computer, from the menu, navigate to **Start| Control Panel | System | Device Manager**. There you need to find the name of the connected device with the record **ADB Interface**. If you cannot find this record, it means that the device drivers were installed incorrectly.

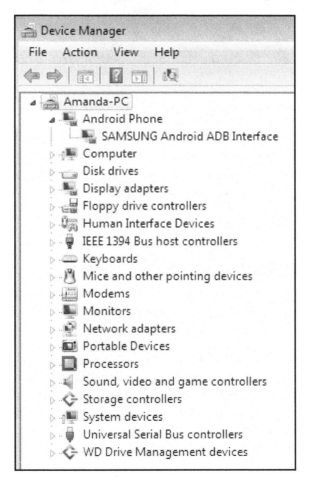

Connected Samsung device running Android operating system

Android Debug Bridge is a command-line utility, which is a part of Android SDK Platform. You can perform connection diagnostics and other manipulations with Android devices via this utility. When the Android SDK Platform program is installed, enter the adb devices command in the Windows Command Prompt. If there are any Android devices connected to the computer, their list will be displayed on the screen.

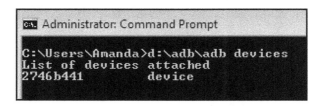

List of connected Android devices

If the device is not detected by the computer, follow these steps:

1. Switch the device connection mode from **Charge only** to **MTP** or **PTP**.
2. Tick **Mock locations** in the **Developer Options** section of the examined device.
3. Tick **Unknown sources** in the **Security** section of the examined device.
4. Disable antiviruses on the examined device.
5. Change the data cable.

Manual assembling of ADB driver

There are no drivers for some Android devices. For such devices, a driver can be created automatically by the programs, such as Oxygen Forensic or Magnet Acquire, but also the driver can be assembled manually. Perform the following steps to do so:

1. Connect the device for which you need to create a driver.
2. Upload Google USB Driver and unpack the uploaded archive.
3. In the unpacked archive, find the android_winusb.inf file and open it in Notepad, which you should run as administrator. You will find the following fragment of text in the file:

```
;Google Nexus One
%SingleAdbInterface%          = USB_Install, USB\VID_18D1&PID_0D02
%CompositeAdbInterface%       = USB_Install, USB\VID_18D1&PID_0D02&MI_01
%SingleAdbInterface%          = USB_Install, USB\VID_18D1&PID_4E11
%CompositeAdbInterface%       = USB_Install, USB\VID_18D1&PID_4E12&MI_01
```

4. Run the Device Manager and find the device (Android or Android Composite ADB Interface).
5. Click the right mouse button.
6. In the opened menu, select **Properties**, then in the opened window select **Details**.
7. In the drop-down **Property** menu, select **Hardware Ids**.

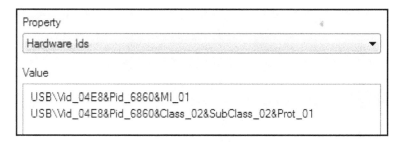

List of Hardware Ids Android devices

8. Replace **Google Nexus One** with the name of your device. Replace the found fragment of text as follows:

```
;Your device name
%SingleAdbInterface%        = USB_Install, USB\VID_04E8&PID_6860
%CompositeAdbInterface%     = USB_Install, USB\VID_04E8&PID_6860&MI_01
%SingleAdbInterface%        = USB_Install, USB\VID_04E8&PID_6860
%CompositeAdbInterface%     = USB_Install, USB\VID_04E8&PID_6860&MI_01
```

9. Save the edited file.
10. In **Device Manager**, select the **Android device**.
11. Click the right mouse button. In the opened window, select **Update Driver Software**.
12. In the next window, select **Browse my computer for driver software** and specify the path to the folder where the edited file `android_winusb.inf` is located.
13. There is a possibility that you will receive messages during the installation of the driver that the driver is incompatible and its installation is not recommended. Continue the installation of the driver. When the installation is finished, reboot the computer.

See also

- The Android Debug Bridge webpage at `https://developer.android.com/studio/command-line/adb.html`.
- Get the Google USB Driver at `https://developer.android.com/studio/run/win-usb.html`.

Android device acquisition with Oxygen Forensic

The program Oxygen Forensic has been already described previously in Chapter 1. In this chapter, the physical dump of a device via Oxygen Forensic will be shown. In order to make a physical dump, you need to have superuser's permissions. You need to gain root access to the device in order to get superuser's permissions. There are many ways to gain the root access at the Android device, `the description of which is beyond the scope of this book`. A special feature of Oxygen Forensic is that before the physical dump is made, the program tries to gain the root access automatically by means of consistent usage of different types of exploits. This function does not lead to any damage of the device. On one hand, this function is a great virtue, but on the other hand, it can be used only for a limited range of devices. On the internet, many methods of gaining root access for a great number of devices are described, but there is a possibility that applying these methods can lead to the damage of the device beyond recovery even before the data extraction.

How to do it...

1. In the Oxygen Forensic program, click on the **Connect device** button that is located on the toolbar. It will start Oxygen Forensic Extractor.

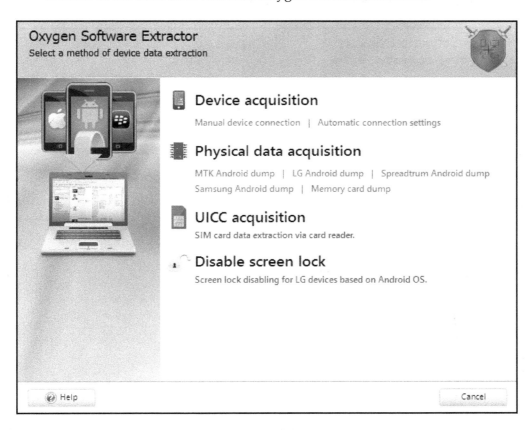

Main window of Oxygen Forensic Extractor

2. Click on **Device Acquisition**. The program will automatically search for the connected device. If the program detects it, then its properties will be shown in the program window. If the device was not detected, you can use the **Manual device connection** and **Automatic connection setting** options in order to try to connect the examined device manually.

The Oxygen Forensic Extractor window with information about a connected device

3. Click on the **Next** button. In the next window, you need to fill in the details of the case, such as **Device alias**, **Case number**, **Evidence number**, **Place**, **Incident number**, **Inspector**, **Device owner**, **Owner email**, and so on.

4. Do not tick the **Parse applications databases and collect data for analytical sections ...** and **Search and recover deleted data ...** options as these actions will take additional time.

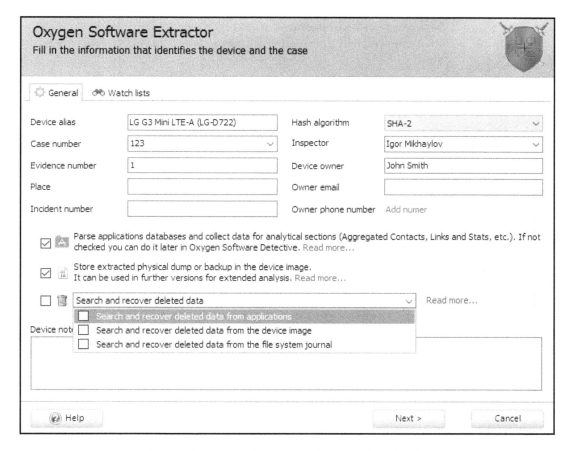

The Oxygen Forensic Extractor window with the case information and extraction options

5. Click on the **Next** button. In the next window, you will be asked to select the data extraction mode.

6. In **Default mode**, the program will attempt to perform the following actions sequentially:

    1. Gaining access to the root of the device. If the root access is gained, the program will go to step 2. Otherwise, it will go to step 3.

    2. Making a physical dump. If this step is successfully completed, then the program will finish its work. Otherwise, the program will go to step 3.

    3. Backup creation. If this step is successfully completed, then the program will finish its work. Otherwise, the program will go to step 4.

    4. Logical extraction from the device. Step 4 is available only for the devices running Android 4.0 or higher.

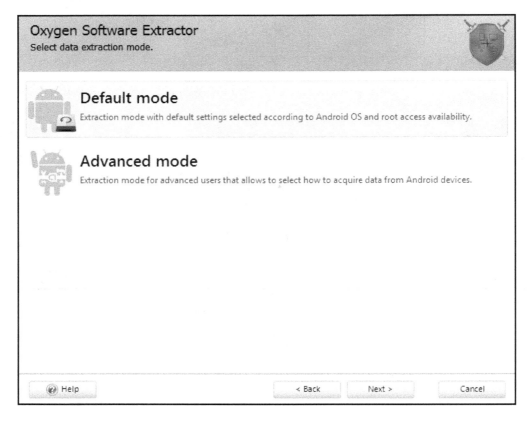

The Oxygen Forensic Extractor window with the options of modes of Android device data extraction

7. In **Advanced mode**, the program prompts you to select the data extraction method. Tick the selected method and click on the **Next** button. Here, we tick **Physical dump** and **Allow rooting** and then click on the **Next** button.

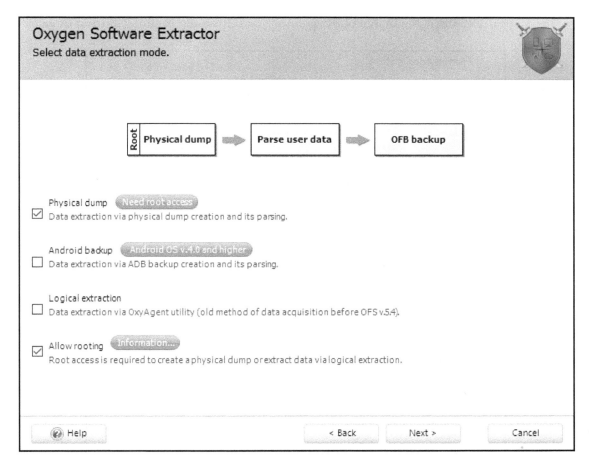

8. The program will prompt you to check the entered data once again by displaying it in the window. If all the data is correct, click on the **Extract** button. The process of creating the physical dump will start.

9. When the extraction is finished, the created case can be opened in the Oxygen Forensic program.

10. If you click on section **Device Information** in the case of having opened via Oxygen Forensic, then you will be able to find information about the created physical dump in the **Device Extended Information** section of the opened window. The mmcblk0 file is the physical dump of the Android device. The mmcblk1 file is the image of the memory card installed on this Android device.

⊟ **Common information**	
Alias	LG G3 Mini LTE-A (LG-D722)
Retail name	LG LG G3 Mini LTE-A (LG-D722)
Manufacturer	LG
Internal name	LG-D722
Platform	Android OS
IMEI	355403061974108
Software revision	5.0.2
Rooted	Yes
IMSI	N/A
S/N	LGD722c8632211
⊟ **Device extended information**	
Device image	mmcblk0
Device image	mmcblk1
⊟ **Extraction information**	
Acquisition type	Android physical image
Extracted by version	9.2.1.71
Extraction started	20.04.2017 18:43:38
Extraction finished	20.04.2017 19:12:08
Extraction duration	00:28:30
Hash algorithm	SHA-2

A fragment of the window section Device Information

11. If you double-click on a file name (mmcblk0 or mmcblk1), then Explorer opens the folder with this file.

How it works...

Oxygen Forensic extracts data from the connected Android device. In this case, depending on the extraction settings, you can create: physical dump, backup, or extract logical data. Data extracted from the device can be analyzed immediately or later.

There's more...

A physical dump can be created by the `dd if = / dev / block / partition's name of = / sdcard / NAME_partition.img` command. The names of the device partitions can be viewed by the adb utility. Data and user files are stored in the `userdata` partition.

See also

- The website where you can find articles about different ways of Android devices rooting: `https://forum.xda-developers.com`

Android device acquisition with MOBILedit Forensic

The best mobile forensic software, such as: UFED (Cellebrite), Oxygen Forensic, XRY (Micro Systemation), Secure View (Susteen), MOBILedit Forensic can extract data from Android devices by installing an agent program on the device. It allows to make logical extraction of data from a device.

We will use the MOBILedit Forensic program to demonstrate this method of data extraction. This program has been described in the `Chapter 1`, *SIM Cards Acquisition and Analysis*.

How to do it...

Let's now explore Android device acquisition with MOBILedit Forensic:

1. When you start the program MOBILedit, the main window of the program displays information about the connected device.

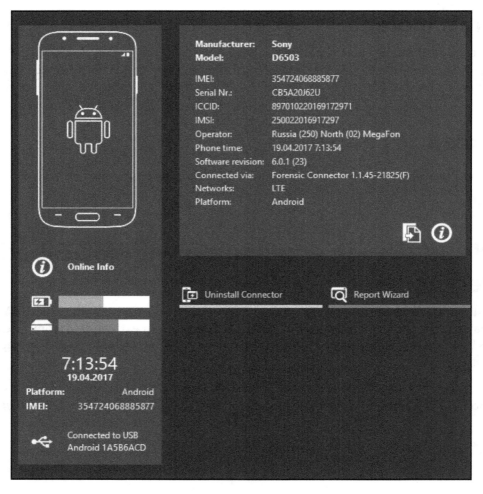

A fragment of the main window with information about the Android device

2. Click on **Report Wizard**. It will open **MOBILedit Forensic Wizard**, which will extract data from the SIM card and generate a report.

3. Fill in the fields: **Device Label**, **Device Name**, **Device Evidence Number**, **Owner Phone Number**, **Owner Name**, and **Phone Notes**. Click on the **Next** button.

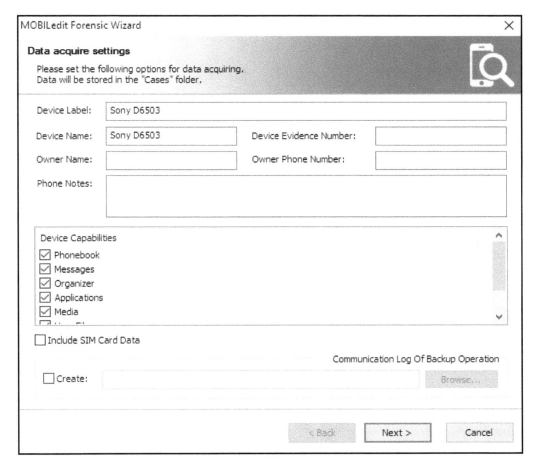

The MOBILedit Forensic Wizard window

4. The data will be extracted. The extraction status will be displayed in the **MOBILedit Forensic Wizard** window. When the extraction is complete, click on the **Next** button.

5. Then, **MOBILedit Forensic Wizard** will display the following window:

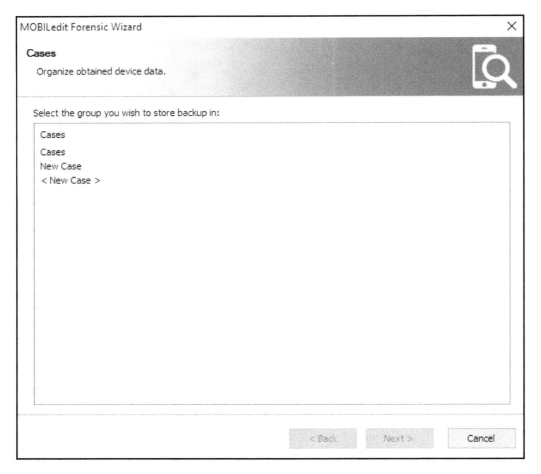

The MOBILedit Forensic Wizard window

6. Click on **<New case>.** In the opened window, fill in the fields **Label, Number, Name, E-mail, Phone Number**, and **Notes**. Click on the **Next** button.

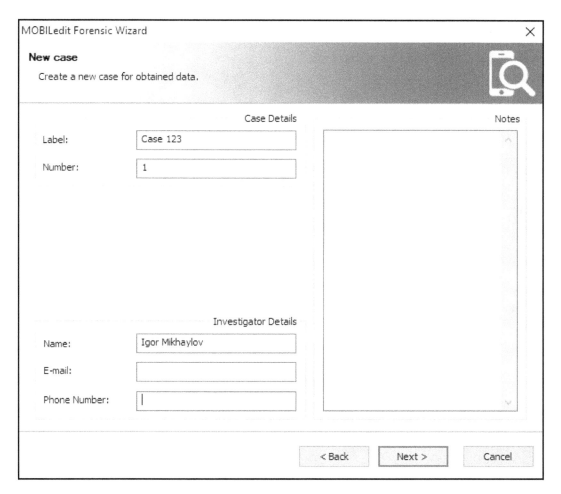

The MOBILedit Forensic Wizard window

7. In the next window of **MOBILedit Forensic Wizard**, select the format in which the report will be generated and click on the **Finish** button.

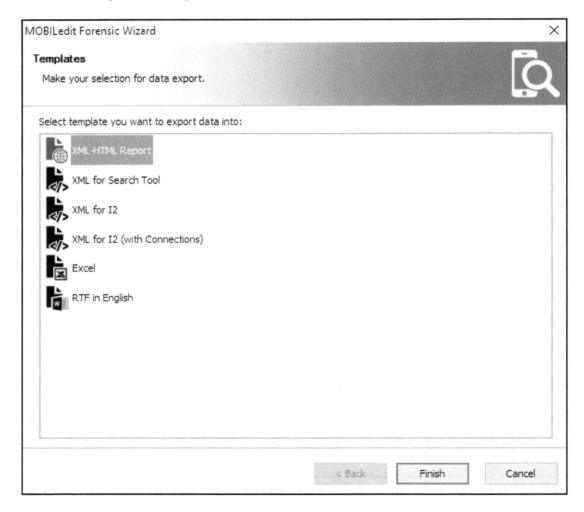

The final window of MOBILedit Forensic Wizard

The forensic report about the extraction will be generated in the selected format.

How it works...

MOBILedit Forensic scans the connected devices. If an Android device is detected, MOBILedit Forensic uploads an agent program **Forensic Connector** in it, and using this agent program, it extracts data from the device. When the extraction is complete, the program will offer to generate a forensic report that will contain all the information extracted from the device.

There's more...

The program MOBILedit Forensic allows to read the data of the SIM card installed in the mobile device. However, it is not recommended, due to the fact that it is impossible to recover deleted records. The correct way is to remove the SIM card from the mobile device and examine it separately.

If you need to analyze the mobile applications data, you need to use not *MOBILedit Forensic*, but the *MOBILedit Forensic Express* program from the same developer.

See also

- The MobilEdit Forensic website: http://www.mobiledit.com
- The MobilEdit Forensic download page: http://www.mobiledit.com/download-list/mobiledit-forensic

Android device acquisition with Belkasoft Acquisition Tool

Belkasoft Acquisition Tool is a universal utility that allows you to create forensic copies of hard disks and mobile devices and extract data from cloud storages. You can get the program by filling in a short form on the developer's website. After that, you will receive an email with a link to download this program.

Getting ready

Download the archive and unpack the program. Connect the examined device to the computer. Click on the BAT icon.

How to do it...

1. In the main window of the program, click on the **Mobile device** icon.

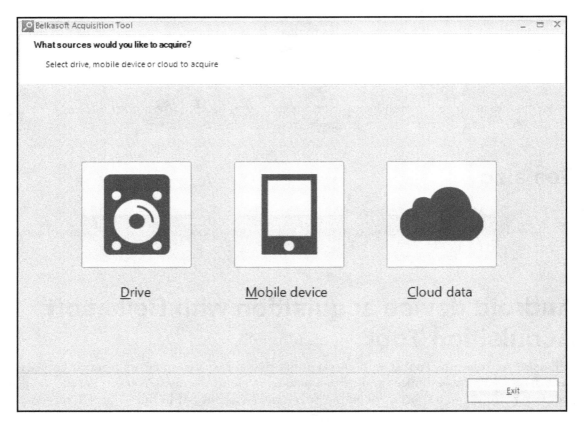

The main window of the Belkasoft Acquisition Tool program

2. In the next window, click on the **Android** icon.
3. In the next window, you can view information about the connected device. Specify the path where the data extracted from the mobile device will be saved. Tick **Copy system applications data**, **Copy SD card content**, and **Copy. apk files (application binaries)** in order to specify what kind of data has to be extracted.

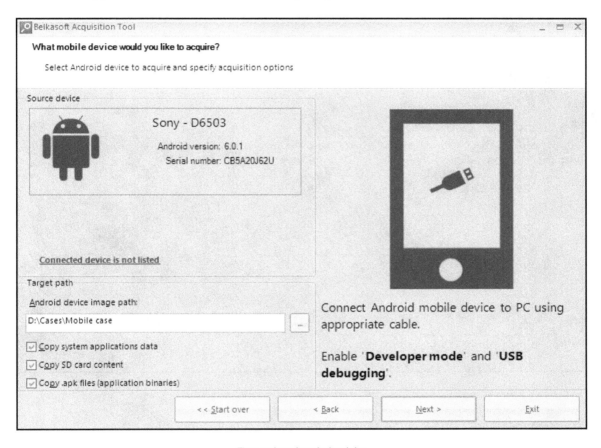

The extraction options selection window.

4. Click on the **Next** button. The data will be extracted from the mobile device. If the device prompts to create a backup, click on **BACK UP MY DATA**.

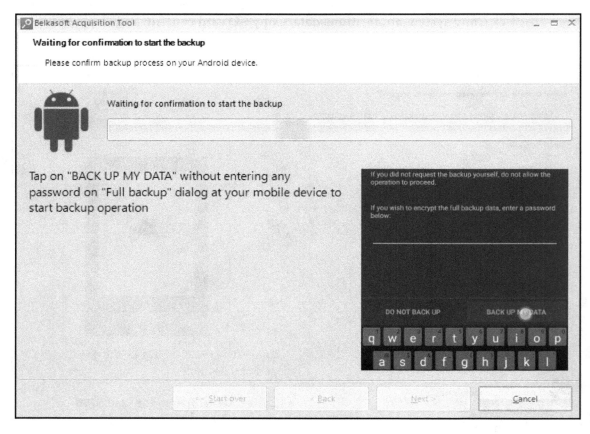

Waiting for the confirmation to start the backup

5. When the extraction is complete, the summary information about the extraction will be displayed. Click on **Open target folder** to go to the folder with the extracted data or click on **Exit** to close the program.

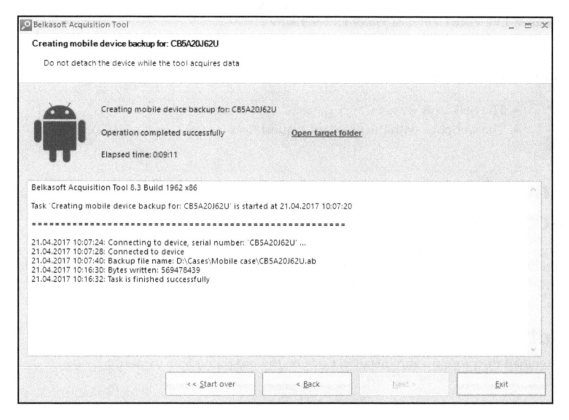

The summary information about the extraction

How it works...

Belkasoft Acquisition Tool scans connected devices. If an Android device is found, the program creates a backup and also extracts other data. This backup can be analyzed via Belkasoft Evidence Center or via other forensic software.

See also

- The Belkasoft website: http://belkasoft.com/
- The webpage with the program request form: http://belkasoft.com/get

Android device acquisition with Magnet Acquire

Magnet Acquire is a free utility designed to create cquire">forensic images of hard drives, memory cards, phones, and tablets. It can be downloaded from the Customer Portal on the Magnet Forensics website. Also, it comes with AXIOM and internet Evidence Finder.

Getting ready

Download the program and install it. Click on the program's icon to start it.

How to do it...

1. Once started, Magnet Acquire looks for connected devices and displays their list in the window.

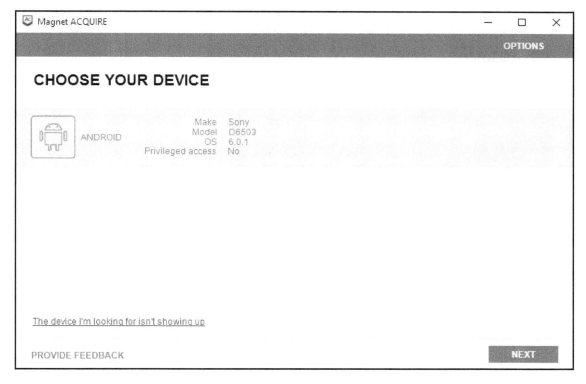

A list of devices displayed in the Magnet Acquire

2. Click on the **NEXT** button. The next window will prompt you to select the type of extraction. Select **Full** if the connected Android device is rooted. Otherwise, select **Quick**.

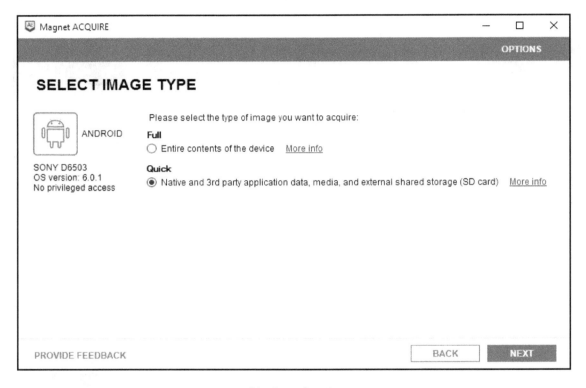

Select the type of extraction

3. Click on the **NEXT** button. If necessary, fill in the **Evidence folder name**, **Folder destination**, **Image name**, **Examiner**, and **Evidence number** fields.

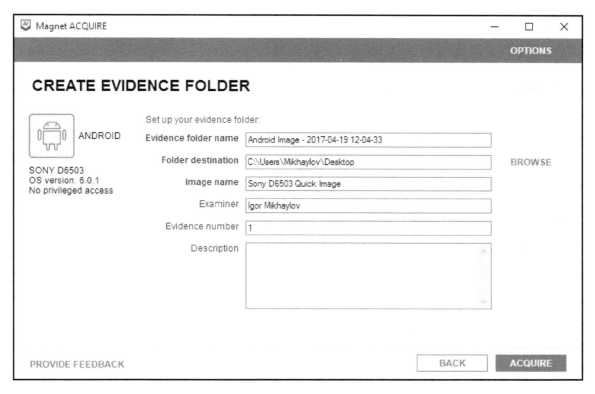

The create evidence folder window

4. Click on the **ACQUIRE** button. The process of data extraction from the device will start.

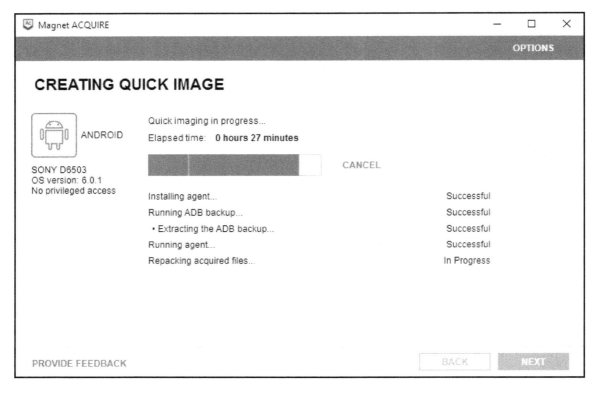

The process of data extraction.

5. When the data is extracted from the device, click on the **EXIT** button to close the program. If you want to go to the folder with the extracted data, click on **OPEN FOLDER.**

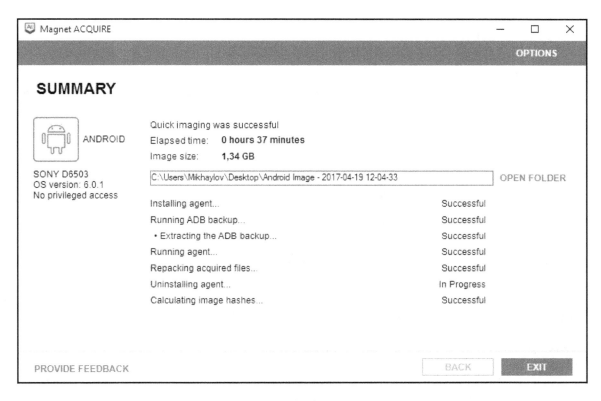

The final window of the program

How it works...

Once started, the program scans the devices connected to the computer and displays their list in the window. There are two ways to extract data using Magnet Acquire:

- If the device is rooted, you can create a physical dump
- If the device is not rooted, a backup of the device is created and all the files that are in the memory card of the device are extracted

Magnet Acquire installs the **ACQUIRE** agent program to extract files from the memory card.

There's more...

If you want the agent program to be automatically deleted after the data extraction, click on **OPTION**. In the drop-down box, select the **Preferences** option. In the opened **Preferences** window, tick **Remove agent application from device after Magnet ACQUIRE is finished.**

See also

- The Magnet Forensics website at https://www.magnetforensics.com/.

Making physical dumps of Android device without rooting

It may seem unusual, but it is possible to make a physical dump of an Android device without rooting and it does not require JTAG and Chip-off methods. It can be done with the devices produced by LG and Samsung and also with the devices with the MediaTeck and Spreadtrum processors. As an example, we will consider the process of making a physical dump of an Android device, produced by LG company, using the Oxygen Forensic. The program Oxygen Forensic has been already described previously in Chapter 1, *SIM Cards Acquisition and Analysis*.

Getting ready

Charge the battery of the device fully and switch it off. Download and install the **Oxygen Forensic** program. This program was described in Chapter 1, *SIM Cards Acquisition and Analysis* and earlier in this chapter in the *Android devices acquisition with Oxygen Forensic* recipe.

How to do it...

1. In **Oxygen Forensic**, click on the **Connect device** button located on the toolbar. It will start **Oxygen Forensic Extractor**.

Physical data acquisition

MTK Android dump | LG Android dump | Spreadtrum Android dump
Samsung Android dump | Memory card dump

A fragment of the Oxygen Forensic Extractor main window

2. In the **Physical data acquisition** window, click on **LG Android dump**. Follow the instructions that appear in the **Oxygen Forensic Extractor** window.

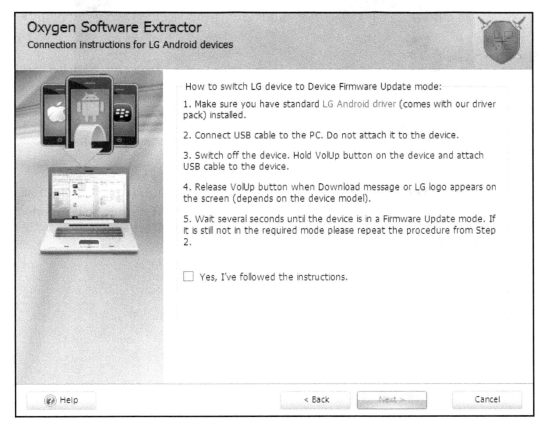

The instructions appear in the Oxygen Forensic Extractor window

3. When Step 5 of the instructions is complete, the following picture will be displayed on the screen of the device:

Firmware Update message on the screen of the device

4. Then, tick **Yes, I've followed the instructions...** and click on the **Next** button.
5. Next, the program will look for the connected device. If the device is detected, the information about the device will be displayed in the **Oxygen Forensic Extractor** window.

Window with information about the connected device

6. Click on the **Next** button.

All the follow-up steps of data extraction from the device are similar to the steps described in the *Android devices acquisition with Oxygen Forensic* recipe in this chapter.

How it works...

A physical dump is made using commands, according to the LG Advanced Flash (LAF) protocol, in the **Firmware Update** mode. Initially, the LAF technology was developed for LG service centers. It allowed to recover LG mobile devices, which do not turn on and do not react to attempts to turn them on (mobile devices drop into this state when users try to gain more privileges in their operating system or in case of errors in updating the system software produced by unqualified users). However, there are a lot of utilities exploiting this technology in non-specialized service centers; these utilities are used for flashing the custom recovery of modified firmware of LG mobile devices.

There's more...

If the LG device does not switch to the **Firmware Update** mode, double-click on the up key when you connect the cable. It is an other way to switching the LG device to to the **Firmware Update** mode.

Unlocking locked Android device

There are different methods of unlocking locked Android devices. Some of them delete the file that contains the lock password of the device by some means or other. In this chapter, you will learn how to delete this file by flashing the modified firmware on the Samsung GT-I9300 smartphone.

For successful flashing of the modified firmware, the bootloader of the device has to be unlocked. If the bootloader is locked, it can be unlocked via a hardware device--flasher. As a rule, different models of flashers are used for mobile phones produced by different companies.

Getting ready

Charge the battery of the device. Download the Odin program. Download and unpack the modified firmware.

How to do it...

1. Switch off the smartphone.
2. Boot the device into the downloading mode by pressing volume down and home buttons and then the power button.
3. You will see the disclaimer; press volume up to continue.
4. Plug in the device and start **Odin**.
5. Click on AP button and choose the tar file with the custom recovery.

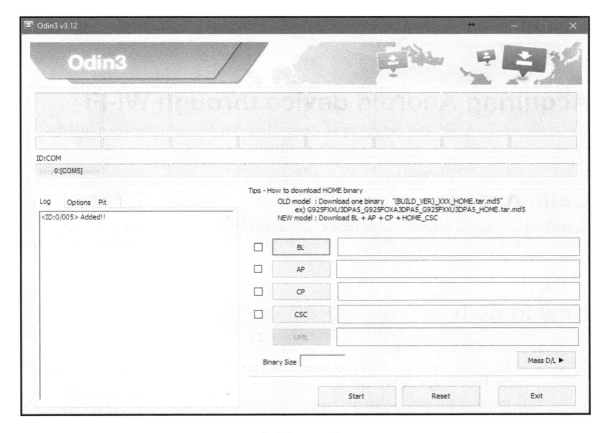

The Odin program window

6. Click on the **Start** button. Wait for the message about successful completion of the firmware to flash. The smartphone will reboot when the flashing is finished.

How it works...

While the message is flashing, the contents of the system partition are replaced. As a result, the file containing the lock password is deleted.

See also

- The web page with the modified firmware: http://www.x-mobiles.net/engine/go.php?url=aHR0cHM6Ly95YWRpLnNrL2Qvc2hNbS1xb1BuTVhraA%3D%3D
- The webpage of the Odin program: https://forum.xda-developers.com/galaxy-s3/themes-apps/27-08-2013-odin-3-09-odin-1-85-versions-t2189539

Acquiring Android device through Wi-Fi

This method allows to extract data from an Android mobile device in case the mini-USB port is damaged and you cannot connect the device to the computer with a cable.

Getting ready

Download and install **MOBILedit Forensic**. This program has been already described previously in Chapter 1 and in this chapter in the *Android devices acquisition with MOBILedit Forensic* recipe.

How to do it...

1. Start MOBILedit Forensic.
2. In the main window of the program, click on **Connect**. In the opened window of MOBILedit Forensic Wizard, select the Android device and then click on **Next**.
3. In the next window, select the type of the device connection with the computer: Wi-Fi.

4. Next, a window with instructions for downloading the **Forensic Connector** mobile application will be displayed.
5. Download **Forensic Connector** to the examined device from Google Play or use the QR code.

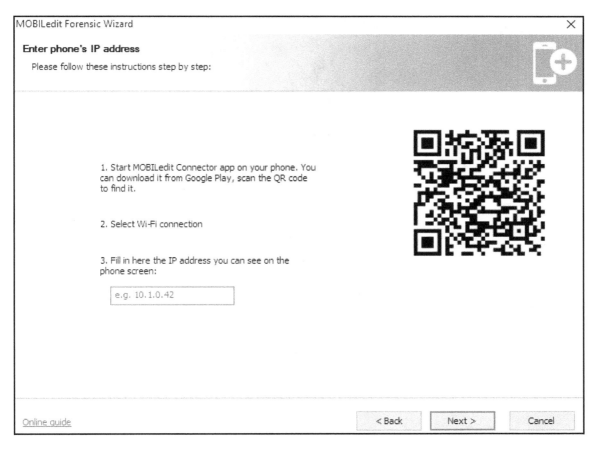

Instructions for downloading the Forensic Connector mobile application

6. Start **Forensic Connector** on the device.

Main window of Forensic Connector

7. Select the type of device connection with the computer: Wi-Fi.

8. Enter the IP address displayed on the device screen in the corresponding field of **MOBILedit Forensic Wizard.** Enter Phone's IP address as shown in the Instructions for downloading the Forensic Connector mobile application image:

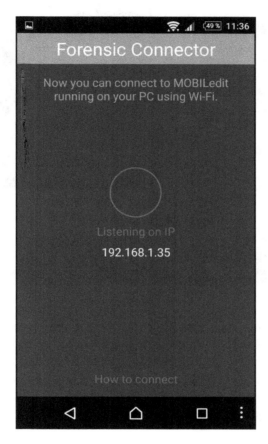

Forensic Connector window with the IP address

9. After this, the authorization confirmation code will be displayed both in **MOBILedit Forensic** and **Forensic Connector**. If the code values in the programs match, click on **Allow.**

Authorization confirmation code

10. When the mobile device and the computer are connected, the procedure of the device's data extraction is similar to the procedure described in the *Android devices acquisition with MOBILedit Forensic* recipe of this chapter.
11. The extraction process will be displayed on the screen of the mobile device.

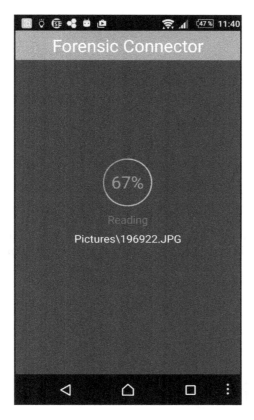

The data extraction process

How it works...

Data extraction from the Android device is carried out through Wi-Fi using the Forensic Connector program installed in the device.

See also

- A description of data transferring via Wi-Fi on the webpage of ADB: `https://developer.android.com/studio/command-line/adb.html`
- The Android ADB webpage: `http://totalcmd.net/plugring/android_adb.html`

Samsung Android device acquisition with Smart Switch

Smart Switch is a canned utility of Samsung for creating backups of modern Samsung devices. Smart Switch replaced Kies, which is currently used to create backups of older Samsung devices. The specific feature of Smart Switch is that it can be used for data extraction from a Samsung device even if the USB Debugging function is not activated in the device. As a rule, Smart Switch is used when there is no other way to extract data.

Getting ready

Go to the web-site of the program (`https://www.samsung.com/us/smart-switch/`). There you can find versions of the program both for PC and for MAC available for downloading. Select the version you need and click on it. When the program is downloaded, double-click on the downloaded file. The installation of the program will start.

How to do it...

1. If the Samsung device is not connected or the device driver is not installed, after starting the program, you will see an animated picture suggesting to connect the device.

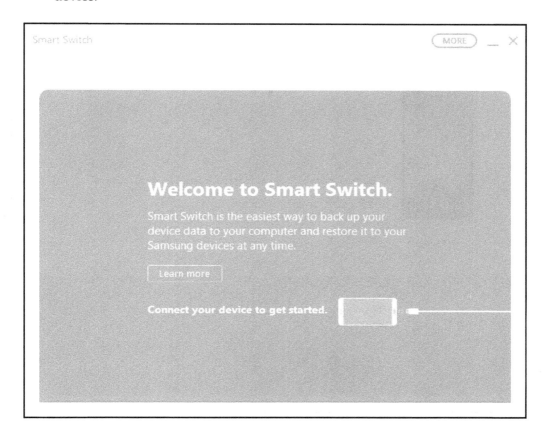

2. If the device drivers are installed correctly and it is connected, you will see a window on which the device model will be displayed. This window will prompt you to make Smart Switch backup or restore Smart Switch backup to the connected device.

The window of the program where the model of the connected device is displayed

3. Click on the **Backup** button. The process of Smart Switch backup creation will start. The creation process will be displayed at the bottom of the window.

The process of Smart Switch backup creation

4. After the creation of Smart Switch backup, the program's window will display the quantity and types of data transferred to the backup.

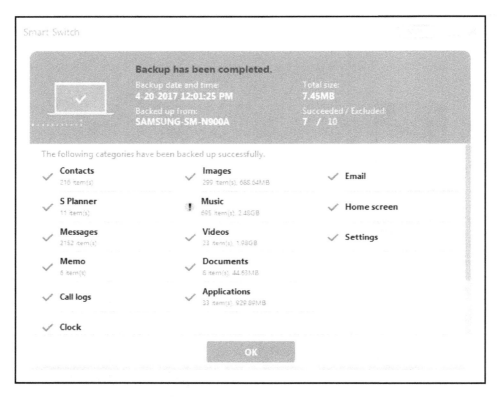

The program's window displaying the quantity and types of data transferred from the device to the Smart Switch backup

How it works...

Smart Switch extracts data from a Samsung device and saves it on a computer. After that, this data can be restored to another Samsung device and then extracted from it by mobile forensic software (such as MOBILedit Forensic, Oxygen Forensic, and so on).

There's more...

1. If Smart Switch can not detect the device in MTP mode, switch it to the PTP mode.
2. Reboot the computer after installation of Smart Switch or device drivers.
3. The created Smart Switch backup is saved to the path: `C: \ Users \% User name% \ Documents \ Samsung \ SmartSwitch`.
4. In the **Check encryption settings** section, you can specify what types of data will be transferred from the device to the backup.

 Unfortunately, there is no forensic program that would support data extraction from Smart Switch backups. Also, part of the information in these backups is encrypted. This is why you cannot view the extracted data manually. In order to extract data from these backups, you need to upload data to the transfer phone. Transfer phone is a rooted Samsung phone after hard reset. After uploading data from the Smart Switch backup into it, the data can be extracted via any forensic program and by any method described in the Chapter.

See also

- The Smart Switch download page at `http://www.samsung.com/us/smart-switch/`.
- The Samsung USB driver for mobile phones at `http://developer.samsung.com/search/searchList.do?searchTop=usb+driver`.

3
Apple Device Acquisition

In this chapter, we'll cover the following recipes:

- Apple device acquisition with Oxygen Forensics
- Apple device acquisition with libmobiledevice
- Apple device acquisition with Elcomsoft iOS Toolkit
- Apple device acquisition with iTunes
- Unlocking a locked Apple device

Introduction

Mobile devices from the Apple company, such as iPhones and iPads, occupy about 15% of the mobile device market. Due to this fact, they often become the object of forensic analysis.

Mobile devices from the Apple company are the most complex objects in forensic analysis. The restrictions of access to the user's data used in the devices do not allow extracting the data in full. The encryption makes the use of all known file recovery algorithms useless. Even if you manage to recover a file in some way, its content will be unavailable, as it will remain encrypted.

The complete examination of an Apple device is possible if you jailbreak it. The file system can be extracted from such a device and via analysis of the file system, you can extract a maximum number of user data. However, this operation cannot be performed for all types of such devices.

For mobile devices up to and including the iPhone 4, you can make physical dumps. It allows you not only to fully extract user's data from devices, but also to recover the screen lock password. You can make physical dumps of Apple mobile devices using forensic programs like UFED Physical Analyzer (Cellebrite), Elcomsoft iOS Forensic Toolkit (Elcomsoft), or XRY (Micro Systemation).

Unlocking locked Apple devices can be a problem, as it is not possible to extract a user's data from a locked device. Apart from the above mentioned method of screen lock password recovery from old Apple devices, there are methods of passwords recovery for the new devices. This function is implemented in software products such as: UFED Physical Analyzer (Cellebrite), Advanced Physical Extractor (Susteen), and also in a hardware solution called IP-BOX. The use of these methods is also limited due to the emergence of additional features in new versions of the iOS operating system that provide even more security.

The unlocking method for locked Apple devices that does not require the purchase of expensive forensic programs or forensic hardware solutions is the use of lockdown files. This method will be described in this chapter.

Alternative sources of information stored on Apple's mobile devices are backups, which can be found on the computers and laptops of device owners and in their iCloud accounts. Often, mobile device owners do not realize that when a mobile device is connected to a computer, the device's backup is automatically created. Due to this fact, the owners of the devices do not take measures to delete such backups.

Apple device acquisition with Oxygen Forensics

The Oxygen Forensics program has been already described previously in Chapter 1, *SIM Cards Acquisition and Analysis* in the recipe *SIM cards Acquisition and Analysis with Oxygen Forensics*. In this chapter, the process of making a logical copy of an Apple mobile device's data via the Oxygen Forensic program will be shown.

Getting ready

In order to extract data from an Apple device, you will need to install the iTunes program, which will also be described in this chapter, in the recipe *Apple devices acquisition with iTunes*. Without iTunes, you can not create the device's backup. The only thing that will be available is the function of copying media files from the device.

How to do it...

1. In the Oxygen Forensics program, click the **Connect device** button located on the toolbar. It will launch Oxygen Forensic Extractor:

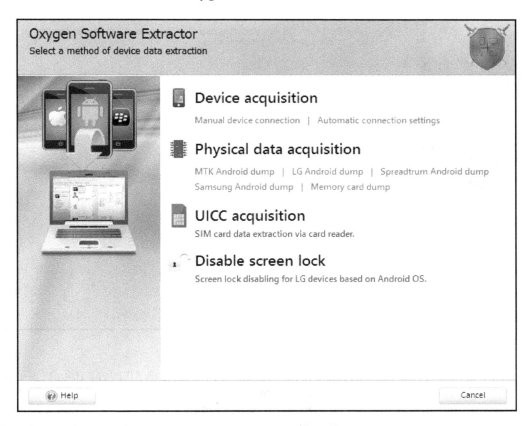

The main window of Oxygen Forensic Extractor

2. Click **Device Acquisition**. The program will automatically search for the connected device. If the program recognizes it, then its properties are displayed in the program's window. If the device is not found, then, using the **Manual device connection** and **Automatic connection setting** options, you can try to connect the examined device manually.

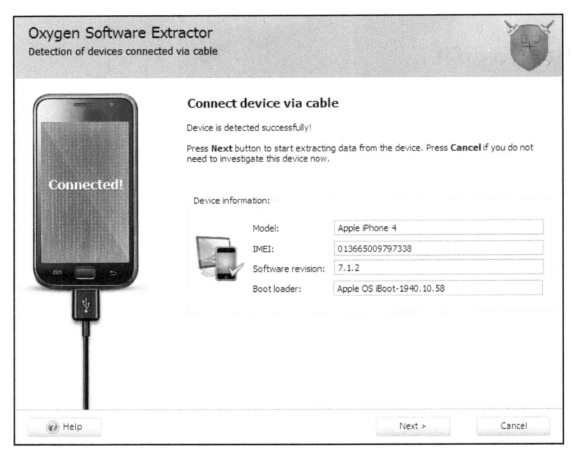

The window of Oxygen Forensic Extractor with information about the connected device

3. Click the **Next** button. In the next window, you need to fill in the details of the case, such as **Device alias**, **Case number**, **Evidence number**, **Place**, **Incident number**, **Inspector**, **Device owner**, **Owner email** and so on. Do not tick **Parse applications databases and collect data for analytical sections...** and **Search and recover deleted data...** as these actions will take additional time.

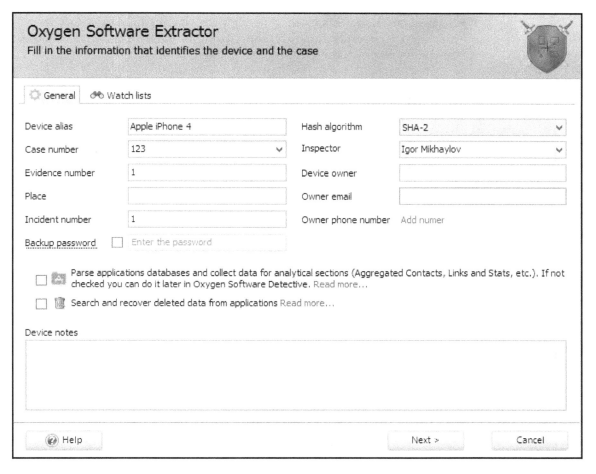

The window of Oxygen Forensic Extractor with information about the case and extraction options

4. Click the **Next** button. In the next window, you will be asked to choose the method of data extraction. Data extraction from Apple's mobile devices is available in two ways:

- **Advanced logical method**: This method implies the use of extended logical protocol instead of the normal iTunes procedure for backup creation. This approach is preferred for data retrieval from non-jailbroken Apple devices with iTunes backups protected by a password (the iTunes password is not required). In order to extract event log and password data, use the classic method.

- **Classic method**: This method implies the standard iTunes procedure of backup creation for data extraction from non-jailbroken Apple devices and data retrieval directly from jailbroken devices.

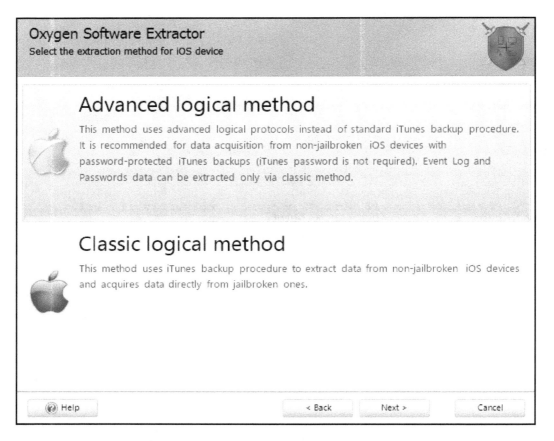

The window of Oxygen Forensic Extractor with the choice of data extraction methods from the Apple device

5. Select the method you need and click the **Next** button.
6. The program will prompt you to check the entered data once again, displaying it in the window. If all the data is correct, click the **Extract** button. The process of backup creation will start.

7. When the backup creation is finished, the procedure of the extracted data analysis will start automatically, after which the data can be viewed in the Oxygen Forensic program.

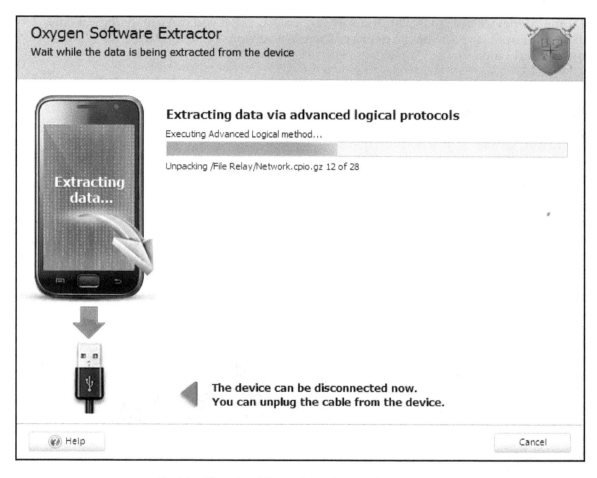

The window of Oxygen Forensic Extractor displaying the progress of the backup analysis

At the end of the extraction, the created case can be opened in the Oxygen Forensic program.

The default password for the encrypted backup created by Oxygen Forensic Extractor is 'oxygen' (without quotation marks).

Apple device acquisition with libmobiledevice

Libmobiledevice is a cross-platform software package that you can use for logical data extraction from Apple's mobile devices. There are versions of this software for Windows, macOS and Linux.

Getting ready

Download the libmobiledevice archive and unpack it.

How to do it...

1. Unlock the device and connect it to the computer.
2. Click **Trust** in response to the request that appears on the screen of your mobile device.
3. Enter the command: `device_id.exe -l`. The `-l` flag is used to get information about all Apple mobile devices connected to the computer. The device UDID was received in response to the request: `1f836c8471c4e60ce771e2fdcf14d7e1b31e8b15`:

```
C:\Users\Igor\Downloads\libmobiledevice>idevice_id.exe -l
1f836c8471c4e60ce771e2fdcf14d7e1b31e8b15

C:\Users\Igor\Downloads\libmobiledevice>_
```

The result of the command device_id.exe -l

4. The device UDID can be used to obtain more information about the connected device. Enter the command: `ideviceinfo.exe -u 1f836c8471c4e60ce771e2fdcf14d7e1b31e8b15`. The result of the command execution will be a large amount of information about the device:

```
C:\Users\Igor\Downloads\libmobiledevice>ideviceinfo.exe -u 1f836c8471c4e60ce771e
2fdcf14d7e1b31e8b15
ActivationState: WildcardActivated
ActivationStateAcknowledged: true
ActivityURL: https://albert.apple.com/deviceservices/activity
BasebandSerialNumber: QUqOWOcesVJYDIeM
BasebandStatus: SIMNotInserted
BluetoothAddress: 98:03:d8:e8:f3:3c
BoardId: 0
BuildVersion: 11D257
CPUArchitecture: armv7
ChipID: 35120
DeviceClass: iPhone
DeviceColor: black
DeviceName: iPhone User
DevicePublicKey: LS0tLS1CRUdJTiBSU0EgUFVCTElDIEtFWS0tLS0tCk1JR0pBb0dCQUsrdzNDdHc
ybFVIa3FjeVJ4UUZmRjBMeHZTT2N4UUhWcHhHM0tIdzR6R6c1UzcGROY2lzR1NpRWYKWkZSY1BsK2VISWF
MZGJYQ2d2RjMrZGU0WGRyeGhHSFRySnBrQm9nTXloTXNDm9zNDB3cFVyen16bGQwRmE2NwpwUTRYaG4
xbEZJaGNyYnhwU1BzdzRSNi9xT2JxRUZJWmdIemNqTFpsUzdMaGs0aUZQaTZqQWdNQkFBRT0KLS0tLS1
FTkQgU1NBIFBVQkxJQyBLRVktLS0tLQo=
DieID: 3314722808593928264
EthernetAddress: 98:03:d8:e8:f3:3e
FirmwareVersion: iBoot-1940.10.58
HardwareModel: N90AP
HardwarePlatform: s5l8930x
HostAttached: true
InternationalMobileEquipmentIdentity: 012655008798149
MLBSerialNumber: J51105H8RDPMG
ModelNumber: MC603
NonVolatileRAM:
  auto-boot: dHJ1ZQ==
  backlight-level: MTU3Mg==
  boot-args:
  bootdelay: MA==
  platform-uuid: AAAAAAAAEACAAJgD2OjzPQ==
PartitionType:
PasswordProtected: false
ProductType: iPhone3,1
ProductVersion: 7.1.2
ProductionSOC: true
ProtocolVersion: 2
ProximitySensorCalibration: UFgDB0AshwLqEjkAtgEGqy8ADwPVbj4AGALnVS0A////////////
////Qg4HAAAADgAAABkAAAAsAAAAIAAAAEAA//////9+
RegionInfo: RR/A
SBLockdownEverRegisteredKey: true
SDIOManufacturerTuple:
  IOSDIOManufacturerID: 720
  IOSDIOProductID: 17193
SDIOProductInfo: P=N90 m=3.1 V=u
SIMStatus: kCTSIMSupportSIMStatusNotInserted
SerialNumber: 70111LMTA4S
SoftwareBehavior: AQAAAAAAAAAAAAAAAAAAAA==
SoftwareBundleVersion:
SupportedDeviceFamilies[1]:
  0: 1
TelephonyCapability: true
TimeIntervalSince1970: 1495098785.730773
TimeZone: Asia/Yekaterinburg
TimeZoneOffsetFromUTC: 21600.000000
TrustedHostAttached: true
UniqueChipID: 43102352653
UniqueDeviceID: 1f836c8471c4e60ce771e2fdcf14d7e1b31e8b15
UseRaptorCerts: false
Uses24HourClock: false
WiFiAddress: 98:03:d8:e8:f3:3d
```

The result of the command execution: ideviceinfo.exe -u 1f836c8471c4e60ce771e2fdcf14d7e1b31e8b15

5. To create a backup of the mobile device, enter the following command:
`idevicebackup2.exe backup D: \ MobileCases \ iPhone_logical.`

6. When the command is entered, the process of file extraction from the mobile device starts. The extraction progress will be displayed in the command window which is as follows:

```
Moving 128 files
[==========================================] 100% Finished
Moving 128 files
[==========================================] 100% Finished
Moving 128 files
[==========================================] 100% Finished
Moving 128 files
[==========================================] 100% Finished
Moving 128 files
[==========================================] 100% Finished
Moving 107 files
[==========================================] 100% Finished
Moving 1 file
[==========================================] 100% Finished
Moving 1 file
[==========================================] 100% Finished
[==========================================] 100% Finished
Removing 1 file
[==========================================] 100% Finished
Removing 1 file
[==========================================] 100% Finished
[==========================================] 100% Finished
Received 12668 files from device.
Backup Successful.
```

The progress of the command idevicebackup2.exe backup D: \ MobileCases \ iPhone_logical

Apple device acquisition with Elcomsoft iOS Toolkit

Elcomsoft iOS Forensic Toolkit is a commercial set of tools allowing you to make various extractions from Apple mobile devices. The following actions can be performed via Elcomsoft iOS Forensic Toolkit:

1. Recovery of the password for a locked Apple mobile device (up to and including iPhone 4).
2. Creation of a physical dump of an Apple mobile device (including the blocked, up to and including iPhone 4).
3. Extraction of the file system of an Apple mobile device (for jailbroken devices).
4. Creation of Apple mobile device backup.
5. And much more.

Elcomsoft iOS Forensic Toolkit supports data extraction from 32-bit and 64-bit Apple mobile devices.

In this chapter, an example of the creation of a physical dump from an iPhone 4 via Elcomsoft iOS Forensic Toolkit will be shown.

Getting ready

Download the program using the link specified in your license and unpack it. Connect a hardware key of Elcomsoft iOS Forensic Toolkit to the computer.

How to do it...

1. Go to the folder with the program and double-click the `Toolkit.cmd` file:

```
              Welcome to Elcomsoft iOS Forensic Toolkit
              This is driver script version 2.20/Win

                   (c) 2011-2017 Elcomsoft Co. Ltd.

Please select an action:
   I   DEVICE INFO       - Get basic device information
   B   BACKUP            - Create iTunes-style backup of the device

   1   ENTER DFU         - Help putting device into DFU mode
   2   LOAD RAMDISK      - Load tools onto the device
   3   GET PASSCODE      - Recover device passcode
   4   GET KEYS          - Extract device keys and keychain data
   5   DECRYPT KEYCHAIN
   6   IMAGE DISK        - Acquire physical image of the device filesystem
   7   DECRYPT DISK
   8   TAR FILES         - Acquire user's files from the device as a tarball
   9   REBOOT            - Reboot the device

   0   EXIT

>:
```

The main window of Elcomsoft iOS Forensic Toolkit

2. Putting an Apple device into DFU mode is a preparatory step for the creation of the physical dump. The script located in step 1 will help you to do it. Press the *1* button. At the confirmation request that will appear, press *Y*. After this step, the instructions on how to put the Apple mobile device into DFU mode will be displayed. Read them carefully. When you are ready, press *Enter*.

3. The script that will sequentially display instructions on the screen of the computer that will help you to put the Apple device into DFU Mode:

```
This script will help you with the timings.

When you are ready press 'Enter' and be prepared to press
Sleep and Home buttons in 3 seconds.

Prepare to push and hold Sleep and Home buttons in
...3...2...1
Push and hold Sleep and Home buttons for
...10...9...8...7...6...5...4
Prepare to release Sleep button while holding Home button
...3...2...1
Release Sleep button but continue to hold Home button for
...10...9...8...7...6...5...4...3...2...1

Release Home button.
```

Script messages

4. The Apple device in DFU Mode looks like it is turned off. There should be no messages displayed on its screen. After that, you can proceed to create a physical dump of the device. If the device's screen was locked before turning off, you need to recover the password using the *3* options from the main window of the Elcomsoft iOS Forensic Toolkit, before the creation of the physical dump of the device.

5. To create the device's physical dump, click *6* in the main window of the Elcomsoft iOS Forensic Toolkit. After that, a custom recovery image will be uploaded and launched in the device. The Elcomsoft logo should appear on the device's screen. If it did not, the examined device might not have been put into DFU mode; try again:

```
            Welcome to Elcomsoft iOS Forensic Toolkit
            This is driver script version 2.20/Win

              (c) 2011-2017 Elcomsoft Co. Ltd.

Detecting device type...
Shutting down iTunes processes.
Checking the device type
Identified device as iPhone3,1
Initializing libpois0n
Shutting down iTunes processes.
Waiting for device in DFU mode to connect...
Found device in DFU mode
Checking if device is compatiblChecking the device type
e with this jailbreak
Identified device as iPPreparing to upload limera1n exploit
hone3,1
Resetting device counters
Sending chunk headers
Sending exploit payload
Sending fake data
Exploit sent
```

The process of the custom recovery image uploading to the device

6. After that, you will be asked to select the partition that should be copied from the device. The user data is located in the user partition:

```
            Welcome to Elcomsoft iOS Forensic Toolkit
            This is driver script version 2.20/Win

              (c) 2011-2017 Elcomsoft Co. Ltd.

Please note that to obtain device disk image you need to load ramdisk
on the iOS device first. If you haven't done this yet, please return
to previous step and use corresponding menu item.

Please select partition to image:
   1   System (rdisk0s1s1) -- this one is NOT ENCRYPTED
   2   User   (rdisk0s1s2) -- this one is ENCRYPTED

   0   Back

>: _
```

The window of partition selection for copying from the device

7. Press number 2. It will start copying data from the partition. The extraction progress will be displayed in the lower left corner of the window. At the end of the extraction, in the program window, summary information about the extraction will be displayed:

```
Save image to file <user.dmg>: user.dmg

rawwrite dd for windows version 0.6beta3.
Written by John Newbigin <jn@it.swin.edu.au>
This program is covered by terms of the GPL Version 2.

13,834M
0+611911 records in
0+611911 records out
13834+1 records in
13834+1 records out
14506401792 bytes (15 GB) copied, 1174.59 s, 12.4 MB/s

Imaging done.

Press 'Enter' to continue
```

Summary information about the extraction

How it works...

When you create a physical dump, a custom recovery image is uploaded into the device's memory. With this custom recovery image, a physical dump, which can contain a system partition or a user partition (or both partitions at the same time), is created.

The custom recovery image is in the device's memory and it does not change the data in the system partition or user partition. In order to delete the custom recovery image, just turn off the device.

See also

- Elcomsoft iOS Forensic Toolkit homepage: `https://www.elcomsoft.com/eift.html`

Apple device acquisition with iTunes

ITunes is a free tool provided by Apple to manage data transfer from the mobile devices of this company. Using it, you can synchronize or transfer media files, create backups of mobile devices, and transfer purchases.

Getting ready

Now let's download iTunes. On the iTunes download page, uncheck **Email me New On iTunes and special iTunes offers.** and **Keep me up to date with Apple news, software updates, and the latest information on products and services..** Click the **Download Now** button. The process of the file downloading will start. When the download is complete, double-click on the file. The installation process of the program will be started.

How to do it...

1. Double click on the iTunes icon. When you first start iTunes, you will be prompted to accept the license agreement, the text of which is displayed in the main program window. Read it carefully and click the **Agree** button.
2. In the next window, also click on the **Agree** button.

3. In the program menu, click **Edit**. In the opened menu, select **Preferences...**. In the opened window, go to the **Devices Preferences** section. Tick **Prevent iPods, iPhones, and iPads from syncing automatically** and **Warn when 5% of the data on this computer will be changed**. In the second inscription, using the drop-down menu, change the value of **5%** to **any**. Click the **OK** button:

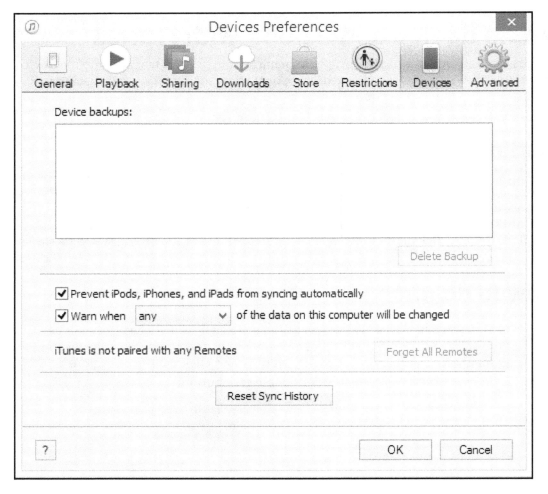

Preferences window

4. Unlock the device and connect it to the computer. Click **Trust** in response to the request that appears on the screen of your mobile device.

5. If, for some reason, you did not allow iTunes to manage the mobile device to the computer, it will show the following box indicating that you forgot to do so:

Window with the message requesting allowance for the computer to manage the mobile device

6. If the computer recognizes the device correctly, you will see a smartphone icon in the upper left corner of iTunes. Click it. No additional software is required to work with the device:

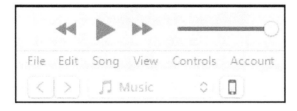

Window with the icon, which indicates that the mobile device was connected correctly

7. The main window of the iTunes program will open, in which the information about the device owner, the status of the device, and so on will be displayed:

Main iTunes window with information about the device

8. In the **Backups** section, tick **This computer** and **Encrypt iPhone backup**. In the opened additional window, enter twice the password that will be used to encrypt the backup. Click the **Set Password** button:

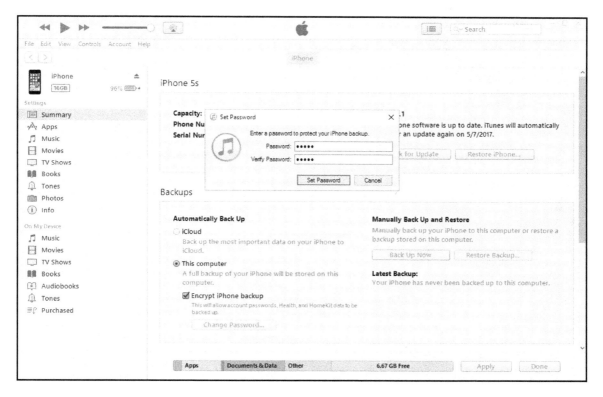

Window for entering the password

9. In the **Backups** section, click the **Back Up Now** button. After it, the process of backup creation for the connected device will start. If an encrypted backup is created, the progress of its creation is displayed in a separate window. If an unencrypted backup is created, the progress of its creation is displayed at the top of the main iTunes window.

The progress of backup creation

10. When the backup creation is finished, the time in the **Backups** section changes to indicate when the backup was created, as shown in the following image:

Information in the latest backup creation section

11. The created backups can be found by the paths:

- Mac OS X - `C:\Users\%username%\Library\Application Support\MobileSync\Backup\` (or `~/Library/Application Support/MobileSync/Backup/`)

- Windows XP - `C:\Documents and Setting\%username%\Application Data\Apple Computer\MobileSync\Backup`

- Windows Vista, 7, 8, and 10 - `C:\Users\%username%\AppData\Roaming\Apple Computer\MobileSync\Backup\`

12. iTunes backups can have different appearances depending on the version of the iOS operating system installed on the examined device:

Name ‸	Date modified	Type	Size
f0	3/13/2017 5:07 PM	File folder	
f1	3/13/2017 5:07 PM	File folder	
f2	12/20/2016 7:21 PM	File folder	
f3	12/20/2016 7:21 PM	File folder	
f4	3/13/2017 5:07 PM	File folder	
f5	3/13/2017 5:07 PM	File folder	
f6	3/13/2017 5:07 PM	File folder	
f7	3/13/2017 5:07 PM	File folder	
f8	3/13/2017 5:07 PM	File folder	
f9	3/13/2017 5:07 PM	File folder	
fa	3/13/2017 5:07 PM	File folder	
fb	3/13/2017 5:07 PM	File folder	
fc	3/13/2017 5:07 PM	File folder	
fd	3/13/2017 5:07 PM	File folder	
fe	3/13/2017 5:07 PM	File folder	
ff	3/13/2017 5:07 PM	File folder	
Info.plist	12/20/2016 7:22 PM	PLIST File	466 KB
Manifest	12/20/2016 7:22 PM	Data Base File	1,704 KB
Manifest.plist	12/20/2016 7:22 PM	PLIST File	31 KB
Status.plist	12/20/2016 7:22 PM	PLIST File	1 KB

Appearance of iTunes backup received for the device with iOS 10 version and higher

Name ▲	Date modified	Type	Size
ffa31951206a42b50dfd8870ede60d5082a10...	5/14/2016 9:04 AM	File	108 KB
ffb022de999740a394faa04f81dea02bb84de...	5/14/2016 9:05 AM	File	38 KB
ffb30a96af99090638b318728d1f87b61bc6b...	5/14/2016 9:04 AM	File	235 KB
ffb361fb137b8a6b638e05fc789f8d8f76517337	5/14/2016 9:05 AM	File	55 KB
ffb8647db025c77e7191c649d4192085d2f4f...	5/14/2016 9:09 AM	File	0 KB
ffba1ba0a54b6833c2e509ee2b5d425b2c2e5...	5/14/2016 9:05 AM	File	12 KB
ffc2dc3539cdb9b427c5e8718562fe17f1bdc0a9	5/14/2016 9:05 AM	File	1 KB
ffc5167c0a0e6b1aa9875f240f8f4ee062a81140	5/14/2016 9:05 AM	File	39 KB
ffcd09f1b3678b3c91a256674b3b40424bc1b...	5/14/2016 9:03 AM	File	2 KB
ffd524c3133a08446ad1393e773885f64e66c...	5/14/2016 9:04 AM	File	1,177 KB
ffd1047cfbb3fe6d859ed6b008b37af8a41e0bf3	5/14/2016 9:03 AM	File	1 KB
ffdad82f93ae3b4d5ca23a80aaf582fad07865f7	5/14/2016 9:04 AM	File	1,112 KB
ffdc480bcda3161ed0f2b801706ab7e4b0c85...	5/14/2016 9:04 AM	File	304 KB
fff8d4731a461d02a5f4d2aca8f398f5806dfba5	5/14/2016 9:05 AM	File	2,873 KB
fffefee216647896ed6ebb73b34d79c84401a...	5/14/2016 9:03 AM	File	0 KB
ffff64402524baf7d1e3bc49780379e69fe69ed0	5/14/2016 9:09 AM	File	1,008 KB
Info.plist	5/14/2016 9:09 AM	PLIST File	2,325 KB
Manifest.mbdb	5/14/2016 9:09 AM	MBDB File	3,180 KB
Manifest.plist	5/14/2016 9:09 AM	PLIST File	36 KB
Status.plist	5/14/2016 9:09 AM	PLIST File	1 KB

The appearance of iTunes backup received for the device with iOS lower than version 10

How it works...

When you connect the unlocked Apple device to the computer, it synchronizes data from your device's memory to your hard drive or iCloud. Depending on the settings selected, the backup can be encrypted or not.

There's more...

If you are prompted to transfer purchases during the process of backup creation, click the **Don't Transfer** button:

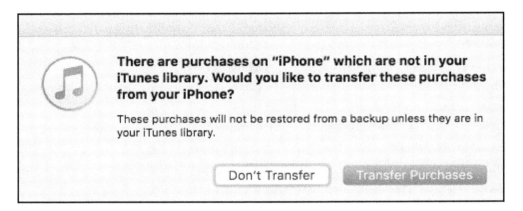

There are purchases on "iPhone" which are not in your iTunes library. Would you like to transfer these purchases from your iPhone?

These purchases will not be restored from a backup unless they are in your iTunes library.

Don't Transfer   Transfer Purchases

Transfer purchases request

The encryption password of the backup entered when the backup is created is stored in the memory of the mobile device. All subsequent backups of the device are automatically created with this password.

See also

- The iTunes download page: https://www.apple.com/lae/itunes/download/

Unlocking a locked Apple device

As was mentioned previously, using lockdown files is the easiest way to unlock any Apple mobile device. An expert can use this method if he does not know the password to unlock the device. The disadvantage of this method is that the expert has to have a computer or a laptop of the device's owner, to which the device was connected before.

How to do it...

Let us now learn how to unlock locked Apple devices:

1. Lockdown files are created by iTunes when an Apple mobile device is connected to a computer - for example, during synchronization of audio files. If an expert has a mobile device and a computer (or laptop) seized from the same person as the mobile device, he can find the lockdown files in the following ways:
    *   Mac OS X – \private\var\db\lockdown
    *   Windows 2000 and XP – C:\Documents and Settings\All Users\Application Data\Apple\Lockdown
    *   Windows Vista, 7, 8, and 10 – C:\ProgramData\Apple\Lockdown

Lockdown files

2. The expert has to copy these files from the examined computer to his computer (to the same folder) for successful data extraction.
3. Now, the data from the mobile device can be extracted via forensic tools, including those described in this chapter.

How it works...

When lockdown files are copied to the expert's computer, the mobile device identifies the expert's computer as the computer to which the device was connected before and therefore allows the transfer of the user's data to it.

There's more...

If the examined device has iOS versions 9 or higher installed, it cannot be unlocked by this method if it was rebooted (or turned off) after the screen lock.

4
Windows Phone and BlackBerry Acquisition

In this chapter, we'll cover the following recipes:

- BlackBerry acquisition with Oxygen Forensic
- BlackBerry acquisition with BlackBerry Desktop Software
- Windows Phone acquisition with Oxygen Forensic
- Windows Phone acquisition with UFED 4PC

Introduction

Mobile devices running Windows Phone OS and Blackberry OS become objects of forensic analysis less and less frequently. The peak of popularity of such devices has already passed. Nevertheless, experts should know methods of data extraction from these devices. These methods will be described in this chapter.

Devices running Windows Phone OS are Microsoft's attempt to enter the mobile devices market with its own OS. Devices running Windows Phone OS appeared on the market in 2010. The majority of these devices were produced by Nokia (which is owned by Microsoft). However, there are models that were produced by such companies as HTC, LG, Lenovo, and Samsung. In order to avoid confusion, it should be remembered that the old versions (7 and 8) of this OS were called Windows Phone. The newest operating system of this family is called Windows 10 Mobile.

BlackBerry was one of the leaders in the production of secure phones. Mainly, the company's own OS, BlackBerry OS, is used on BlackBerry mobile devices. In order to extract data from such devices, an expert needs to know a username and account password (BlackBerry ID). This information is required for data decryption, which is stored in the phone's memory or in its backups.

BlackBerry stopped production of mobile devices running BlackBerry OS in 2015. The Android operating system is now used on new models produced by BlackBerry.

In September 2016, BlackBerry announced the cessation of smartphone production.

BlackBerry acquisition with Oxygen Forensic

Oxygen Forensic was described in `Chapter 1`, *SIM Cards Acquisition and Analysis*. In this chapter, the process of a logical copy of a BlackBerry mobile device data via Oxygen Forensic will be explained. A logical copy contains only certain types of logical data, such as phonebook, calls, messages (SMS, MMS), pictures, and video.

Getting ready

In order to extract data from a BlackBerry device, you need to install Blackberry Desktop Software (this program will be described later).

How to do it...

1. In the Oxygen Forensic program, click the **Connect device** button located on the toolbar. It will launch Oxygen Forensic Extractor.

2. Click **Device Acquisition**. The program will automatically search for the connected device. If the program recognizes it, then its properties are displayed in the program's window. If the device is not found, then using the **Manual device connection** and **Automatic connection setting** options, you can try to connect to the device manually:

The Oxygen Forensic Extractor window with information about the connected device

3. Click the **Next** button. In the next window, the program will request login and password from the device owner's account. This information is necessary to decrypt the data in the memory of the examined device. Check that your workstation is connected to the internet and you have access to the website `https://us.blackberry.com/bbid`:

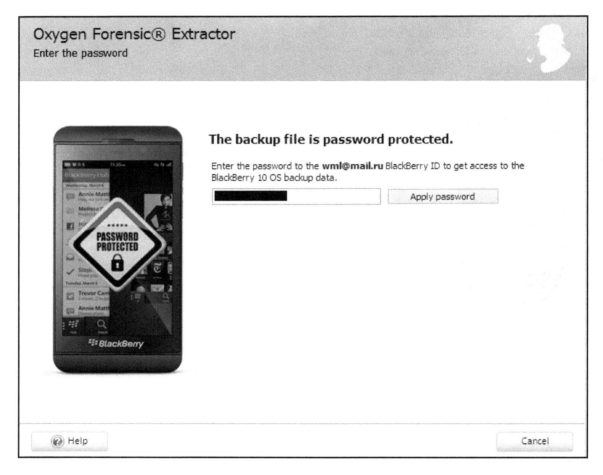

The login window of the device owner's user account

4. Click **Apply password**. If the user's identification details are entered correctly and the program does not display an error message, then click the **Next** button.

5. In the next window, you need to fill in the details of the case, such as **Device alias**, **Case number**, **Evidence number**, **Place**, **Incident number**, **Inspector**, **Device owner**, and **Owner email**. Do not tick **Parse applications databases and collect data for analytical sections...** or **Search and recover deleted data...** because these actions will take additional time.

6. Click the **Next** button. In the next window, you will be asked to select types of data (phonebook, calls, SMS, MMS, media files, and so on). Tick the types of data you want to extract from the device. Click the **Next** button.

7. The program will prompt you to check the entered data once again, displaying it in the window. If all the data is correct, click the **Extract** button. The data extraction process will start.

8. When the extraction is complete, the procedure of the extracted data analysis will start automatically, after which the data can be viewed in the Oxygen Forensic program:

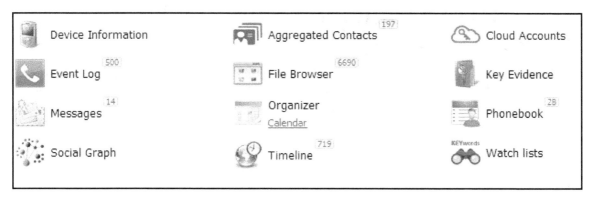

The results of data analysis extracted from the BlackBerry device

There's more...

Despite the fact that BlackBerry OS is outdated, the approaches of BlackBerry regarding data storage with the use of encryption cause a lot of problems for experts.

Even with logical data extraction or data extraction from backups, an expert will need passwords to unlock and decrypt data on the device. In some cases, depending on the version of BlackBerry OS, the username and password from the BlackBerry ID account will be required to decrypt the user data.

The encrypted data on the device is displayed by an additional icon on the device's display.

On devices running operating systems lower than BlackBerry OS 10, the `info.mkf` file (located at `/BlackBerry/system/`) can be found on the memory card installed on the device. This file contains the password, which can be used for backup creation. The `info.mkf` file is created if the device was locked and the data on its memory card was encrypted with the use of the lock password or with the data encryption password. The password from the file can be extracted by third-party utilities.

Sometimes, the examined device can be associated with a **BlackBerry Enterprise Server** (**BES**) account. BES is a program that allows BlackBerry devices to access corporate messaging and collaboration software such as Microsoft Exchange, Lotus Domino, and Novell GroupWise. If the device owner forgot the lock password of the device (or the encryption data of the device), these passwords can be reset by the BES administrator. It should be noted that the user data is not deleted.

BlackBerry acquisition with BlackBerry Desktop Software

Blackberry Desktop Software is an alternative tool that can be used for creating backups of the data on a BlackBerry device. Subsequently, the data from these backups can be extracted by third-party forensic tools. It should be remembered that the data in the backups is encrypted. In order to decrypt the data, you need to have a login and password from the device owner's account.

Getting ready

1. Download BlackBerry desktop software from `https://us.blackberry.com/software/desktop`. Double-click the downloaded file, then the program installation process will start. The following components will be installed:
    * Drivers for BlackBerry mobile devices.
    * **BlackBerry Blend** is a tool that is used for data viewing (such as calendar and contacts) on the device. BlackBerry Blend can be used to transfer files between the device and computer.
    * **BlackBerry Link** is used to create backups of the device and transfer the owner's data to a new device. Also, BlackBerry Link can be used to update the firmware of a Blackberry mobile device. The device can be reset via BlackBerry Link.

2. Read and accept the license agreement, which will be displayed in the Blackberry Desktop Software window, by clicking the **Accept** button. Follow the installation instructions displayed in the Blackberry Desktop Software window.

3. At the end of the installation process, click the **Close** button. Reboot the computer.

How to do it...

1. Unlock the examined device and connect it to the computer. You can check if the device is connected by starting BlackBerry Device Manager. The connected BlackBerry devices will be displayed in its window. The information about the connection to the computer can be also found in the Settings section of the device.

2. Double-click the BlackBerry Link icon. At the first start, the program will prompt you to set it up.

There are no difficulties in these settings. Write down and memorize the path where the backups will be saved. You will be able to see information about the connected BlackBerry device at the third step of the program setup procedure.

3. When the setup is complete, you will see the main program window containing detailed information about the connected device:

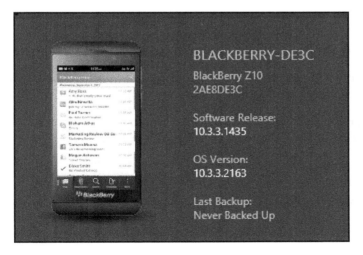

BlackBerry Link window with information about the connected device

4. Double-click the connected device. BlackBerry Link will display the main window, with which you will be able to manage the device:

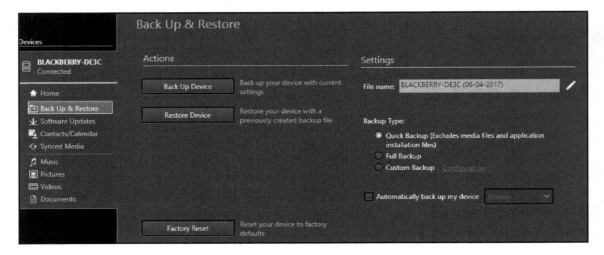

The BlackBerry Link window with options to manage the device

5. Select the backup type that you want to create and click the **Back Up Device** button. The process of creating a new backup of the connected device will start. After the backup is complete, you should extract data of the backup using tools from `Chapter 10`, *Windows Phones and BlackBerry Forensics*.

There's more...

Mobile devices running BlackBerry OS can be connected to the expert's computer with a cable. Depending on the model of the device, mini-USB or micro-USB cables are used.

When connecting the device, make sure that the device is decrypted and unlocked. If the device is locked, it will not be recognized by the computer's OS.

If the device is encrypted, then when it is unlocked, the second password that is used for decryption of the data can be requested. The device's unlock password and the password for data decryption may vary.

When you examine mobile devices running BlackBerry OS, keep in mind that this company was the first one to announce the functionality of remote wiping of user data from the device. Due to this fact, before working with these devices, the expert should take measures to prevent remote control of the device.

The typical mistake of an expert at this step is incorrect driver installation. Let's take a closer look at the process of connecting BlackBerry devices with different versions of the OS to the expert's computer.

Connecting a device running Blackberry OS 5 or 6

The following steps needs to be followed to connect the device having BlackBerry OS 5 or 6:

1. Install the BlackBerry Desktop Software program (`http://blackberry.com/software/desktop.html`) on your computer. This program contains the latest driver versions and the required certificates for the relevant BlackBerry devices.
2. Unlock the device if it is locked with the password.
3. When you connect the device to the computer, you will be prompted to select different connection modes. Do not choose any mode.
4. If there is no connection, try to stop the `BbDevMgr.exe` process in the Task Manager manually.

Connecting a device running Blackberry OS 10

The following steps needs to be followed to connect the device having BlackBerry OS 10:

1. Install the BlackBerry Link program (`http://blackberry.com/software/desktop/blackberry-link.html`) on your computer. This program contains the latest driver versions and the required certificates for the relevant devices.
2. Unlock the device if it is locked with the password.
3. Connect your computer to the internet. It is a requirement as the encryption keys can be obtained only from the BlackBerry server.
4. Enter the BlackBerry ID account username and password associated with the device in Oxygen Forensic Extractor.

See also

- Blackberry Desktop Software homepage: `https://us.blackberry.com/software/desktop`
- BlackBerry ID homepage: `https://us.blackberry.com/bbid`

Windows Phone acquisition with Oxygen Forensic

Oxygen Forensic has been already described previously in `Chapter 1`, *SIM Cards Acquisition and Analysis*. In this recipe, the process of creating a logical copy of a Windows Phone mobile device data using Oxygen Forensic will be shown.

Getting ready

In order to extract data from a Windows Phone device, you should to connect the device both via USB and via the Bluetooth interface (connecting via the Bluetooth interface is not a mandatory requirement to extract data in general. It's only required for extracting contacts.). It will give an opportunity to fully extract user data from the device.

How to do it...

1. In Oxygen Forensic, click the **Connect device** button located on the toolbar. It will launch Oxygen Forensic Extractor.
2. Click **Device Acquisition**. The program will automatically search for the connected device. If the program recognizes the device, then its properties are displayed in the program's window. If the device is not found, then you can try to connect the examined device manually using the **Manual device connection** and **Automatic connection setting** options:

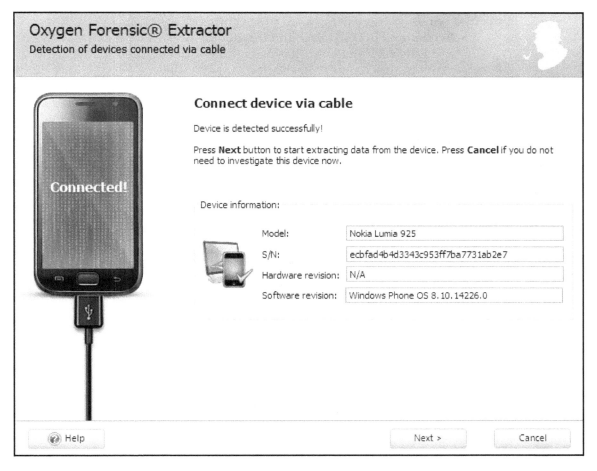

Oxygen Forensic® Extractor

Detection of devices connected via cable

Connect device via cable

Device is detected successfully!

Press **Next** button to start extracting data from the device. Press **Cancel** if you do not need to investigate this device now.

Device information:

Model:	Nokia Lumia 925
S/N:	ecbfad4b4d3343c953ff7ba7731ab2e7
Hardware revision:	N/A
Software revision:	Windows Phone OS 8.10.14226.0

Connected!

Help   Next >   Cancel

Oxygen Forensic Extractor window with information about the connected device

3. Click the **Next** button. In the next window, you need to fill in the details of the case, such as **Device alias, Case number, Evidence number, Place, Incident number, Inspector, Device owner**, and **Owner email**. Do not tick **Parse applications databases and collect data for analytical sections...** or **Search and recover deleted data...** because these actions will take additional time.

4. Click the **Next** button. In the next window, you will be prompted to select the data types (phonebook, calls, SMS, MMS, media files, and so on). Tick the data types that you want to extract from the device. Click the **Next** button.

5. In the next window, you will be asked to select connection type:
    - **Extraction via USB cable and Bluetooth** - This method extract contacts and calls via Bluetooth. Files from flash card and general information about the device will be extracted via USB cable.
    - **Extraction via USB cable** - Only files from the flash card and general information about the device will be extracted via USB cable.

6. Use the first option to extract contacts and calls:

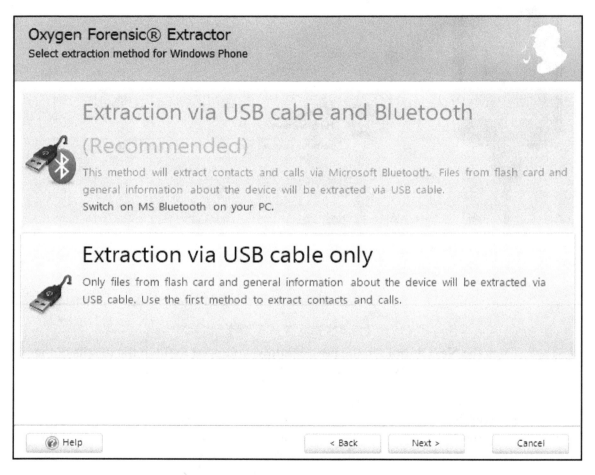

The Oxygen Forensic Extractor window with the data extraction options from a Windows Phone device

7. The program will prompt you to check the entered data once again, displaying it in the window. If all the data is correct, click the **Extract** button. The data extraction process will start.

8. When the extraction is complete, the procedure of the extracted data analysis will start automatically, after which the data can be viewed in Oxygen Forensic.

There's more...

Data stored both in the external storage medium (memory card) and in the internal memory can be encrypted on devices running Windows Phone OS.

Encryption of such devices is implemented on the basis of BitLocker technology using the **Advanced Encryption Standard** (**AES**, 128-bit encryption) encryption algorithm. The cryptographic key is stored on a separate chip, which makes it difficult to extract this key. Access to the data in the device's memory and external storage medium can be additionally blocked by a password on the hardware level. Everything mentioned here taken together makes data extraction from the device very difficult.

The security policies used on these devices do not allow the user to disable encryption or change the encryption algorithm to a simpler one. Conversely, additional options can be included, for example, those that allow to delete user data if a password cracking attempt is detected.

Most of the devices running Windows Phone OS have a slot for a memory card. In Windows Phone version 8, the option that allows installing applications not only to the internal memory but to the memory card appeared. All the applications and data in the memory card are encrypted automatically, but it should be mentioned that media content (pictures and videos) is not encrypted. It allows the device's owner to exchange these kinds of files with other users without any difficulties.

You may need the lock password in order to get access to the device running Windows Phone OS. Users, especially corporate users, are forced to use the password by the rules that were set by the administrators of **Master Data Management** (**MDM**) or Microsoft **Exchange ActiveSync** (**EAS**).

Devices running Windows Phone OS also support the following managing methods:

- **Remote wiping**: The company's technicians can initiate remote device wiping via MDM or the Exchange Server management console. Users can initiate remote device wiping by using the Microsoft **Outlook Web Access** (**OWA**) service.
- **Partial data removal**: If the device is associated with MDM, the system administrator can partially wipe the device. In this case, the corporate data and the settings of corporate accounts are deleted, but the device owner's personal data is saved.
- **Remote lock**: The company's technicians can remotely lock the device. Later, the device can be unlocked.
- **Remote reset of the lock password**: The company's technicians can remotely reset the screen lock password, for example, if the user forgot it. The corporate and personal data of the user are saved.

Windows Phone acquisition with UFED 4PC

Cellebrite company products, such as UFED 4PC, UFED Touch, and UFED Physical Analyzer, are among the best in the field of mobile forensics. In this recipe, the process of data extraction from a Windows Phone device using UFED 4PC will be shown.

Getting ready

A trial license for UFED 4 PC can be obtained by request from Cellebrite distributors. In response to the request, you will receive an email with links to the distributions.

1. Download UFED 4 PC.
2. Double-click the setup file icon.
3. Install UFED 4 PC following the instructions. After installation, click on the UFED 4 PC icon.

   After starting, the program will show a window that indicates that the program is not activated:

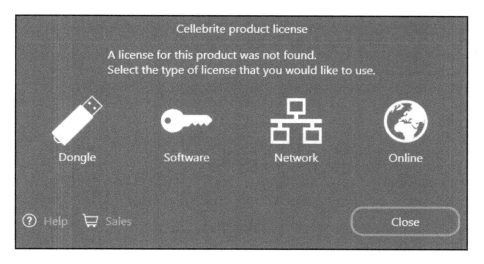

UFED 4 PC window offering to select the type of license

4. Click **Software**. In the new window, the computer ID, which has to be sent to the distributors, will be displayed:

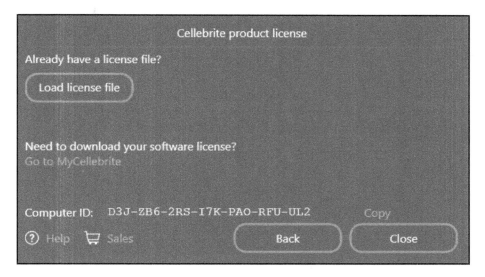

UFED 4 PC window with the computer ID

5. In response to the message with the computer ID, you will receive a message that will contain links to the license files.

To activate your application license, follow these steps:

1. Save the license to your PC.
2. Launch the relevant application.
3. The application will open and a Cellebrite Product Licensing window will appear.

    In the Cellebrite Product Licensing window: **Software | Load license file.**

4. Select the `License` file and click **Open**.
    The Cellebrite Product Licensing window will display the following message: **Your software license has been successfully updated.**
5. Click **Close**.

The application is now activated!

How to do it...

1. Start UFED 4 PC by double-clicking the icon of the program.
    The mobile device can be identified by UFED 4 PC automatically when connected, or it can be done manually.
2. To select the examined device manually, click the **Mobile device** icon. In a new window, select the **Nokia GSM** icon.
3. In the next window, you will be prompted to select the path to save the data extracted from Windows Phone. If you want to select another location to save the data, click **Change target path**. Enter a new path. Click the **OK** button.

4. In the next window, select the type of extraction:

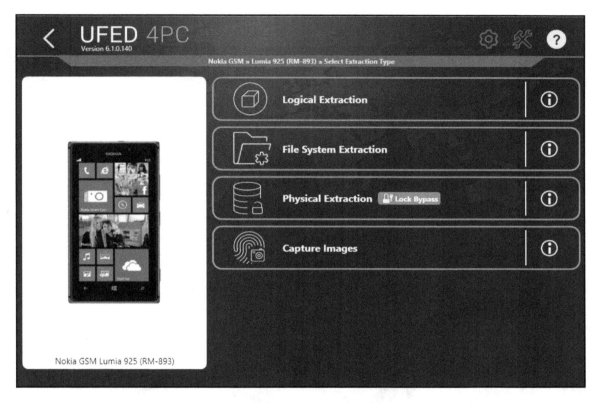

Extraction type selection

5. Click **File System Extraction**. In the next window, you will be provided with the device connection instructions. Connect the device following the instructions. Click the **Continue** button:

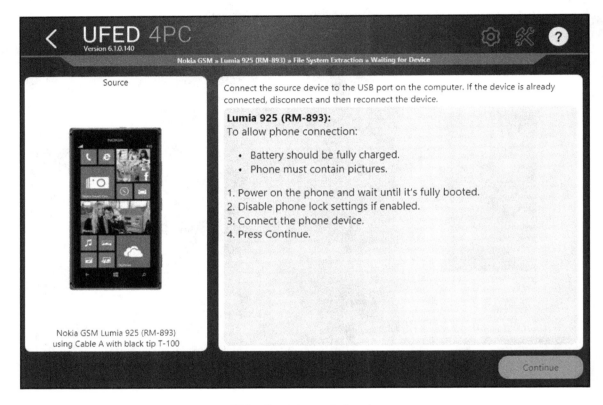

Windows Phone device connection instruction

The process of data extraction from the device will start. At the end of the extraction, the final window will be displayed, in which you will be prompted to choose one of the following:

- Open the extracted data in UFED Physical Analyzer.
- Open the folder containing the extracted data.
- Add another extraction from the same device, but by another method.
- Click the **Finish** button to complete the work.

See also

The homepage of the Cellebrite company: `http://www.cellebrite.com`.

5
Clouds are Alternative Data Sources

In this chapter, we'll cover the following recipes:

- Using Cloud Extractor to extract data from Android devices from the cloud
- Using Electronic Evidence Examiner to extract data from a Facebook account
- Using Elcomsoft Phone Breaker to extract data from iCloud
- Using Belkasoft Evidence Center to extract data from iCloud

Introduction

Nowadays, we can see the emergence of new sources of information that is stored or was stored in mobile devices' memory. The most well-known of them are as follows:

- Google services that store information from mobile devices running Android OS
- Apple cloud storage, iCloud, which stores data from Apple devices
- Microsoft services that store information from mobile devices running Windows Phone OS

What are the features of these services? Owners of Apple devices are limited in the way they manage the data that is saved in iCloud. That is why, if a device owner deleted unwanted information from the device, it can be recovered from the iTunes backup, which is stored in iCloud. In the same way, image files and video files that were permanently deleted from devices can be recovered from iTunes and Android backups.

Microsoft services are used for the synchronization of data between the owner's different devices running Windows. Therefore, this cloud may contain information and documents from the owner's other devices. In other words, if an expert has access to this cloud, they have access to almost all the data on the devices of the person to whom the account in the cloud belongs.

Due to the fact that a huge volume of confidential data is stored in the cloud services, companies (owners of the cloud services) constantly improve the data security mechanisms. Two-factor authentication is used almost everywhere, and it inhibits access to the data. That is why it is especially important that the forensic tools you use for the data extraction from the clouds to support all the mechanisms of user authentication in the examined cloud services.

UFED Cloud Analyzer, produced by Cellebrite, is a very good program used for data extraction from cloud services. The author tested this program and was very pleased with its functionality and the ability to extract data from various cloud services. However, this program is very expensive and, at the time of writing, it was affordable only to military and government organizations. You can get a trial version of the program from regional Cellebrite dealers.

Another interesting tool for working with cloud services is XRY Cloud by Micro Systemation (www.msab.com). However, the author of the book did not manage to get a trial or a full version of this program, which is why I cannot tell you anything about this product.

What should you keep in mind when you work with programs used for data extraction from cloud services? As a rule, these programs can extract data not only with login and password of an account owner, but also with a token. Token usage for data extraction from cloud services has the following advantages:

- There is no need to know the login and password to get access to a cloud storage
- It allows you to bypass two-factor authentication
- A token can be valid from several hours to several months

That is why the faster a mobile device is delivered to a forensic laboratory, the higher the chance of successful data extraction from cloud accounts that are used on the device.

Using Cloud Extractor to extract data from Android devices from the cloud

Oxygen Forensic was described in `Chapter 1`, *SIM Cards Acquisition and Analysis*. This program contains the Cloud Extractor module, which can be used for data extraction from cloud services. To some extent, the interface and functionality of Oxygen Cloud Extractor are similar to UFED Cloud Analyzer. However, Oxygen Cloud Extractor is cheaper than UFED Cloud Analyzer and it is easier to purchase. In this chapter, the data extraction from Google services with the use of Cloud Extractor will be described.

How to do it...

1. First, you need to extract all the logins, passwords, and tokens from the examined device. If you extracted the filesystem or made a physical dump of the device, it increases the probability of success of the necessary data extraction. Remember that user logins and passwords can also work with other cloud service accounts. All you need is to test it.

2. After extracting data from the mobile device, the information about the extracted data that can be used to access cloud services will be displayed on the device's desktop in Oxygen Forensic:

Fragment of the device's desktop, which shows that there were four cloud accounts extracted from the device

3. If you click **Cloud Accounts**, the desktop of the section, where you will see the usernames, passwords, and tokens that you can use to access data stored in the cloud, will open:

Service	Account	Password / Token	Source
Microsoft	████@hotmail.com	Malysh3006	E-mail (http://eas.outlook.com)
Google	████@gmail.com	Malysh3006	E-mail (http://imap.gmail.com)
Google	████@gmail.com	oauth2rt_1/if2pCIGse1nIXXZf7mZhYqDq3CeRGZQh-5BIFan3ocw	accounts.db
Google	████@gmail.com	oauth2rt_1/dADOL9JURnk1S1cD5MoNF89DcLMeJzOOk0ldAAoKWIE	accounts.db

Information about extracted usernames, passwords, and tokens

4. Click on **Extract data** on the toolbar to extract data from cloud services. Fill in the details of the case: **Owner name**, **Owner email**, **Owner phone number**, **Evidence number**, **Incident number**, **Extraction alias**, **Inspector**, **Case**, **Place**, and so on.

5. In the next window, the program will show which services are available for extraction. If you have credentials (or a token) for another cloud service, click **Add credentials** and add them. Click **Next**:

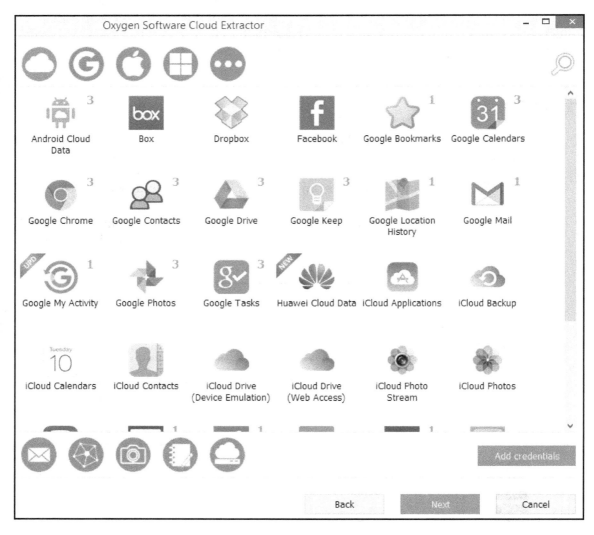

Cloud services available for extraction

6. The program will automatically start the verification process of the entered credentials and tokens. The verification progress will be displayed in the program's window:

The verification process required to access cloud storage

7. If any cloud service requires two-factor authentication, the program will open the additional window and prompt you to enter this data.
8. In the next window, select the range of dates you need. Click **Next**.
9. The process of data extraction from cloud services will start. The data extraction progress will be displayed in the program's window:

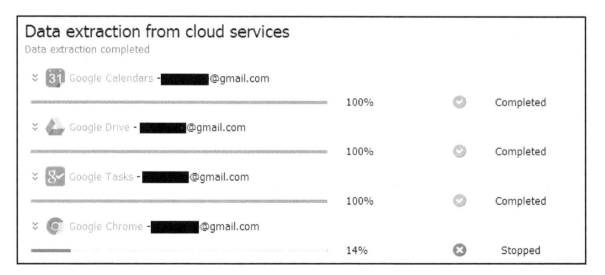

Results of the data extraction from cloud services

10. In the next window, summary information about the extraction will be displayed. Click the **Next** button. Then, the final window of the program will be displayed, which will prompt you to select one of the following actions:
    - **Open extracted data in the Oxygen Software Detective**
    - **Show OCB-backup** (backup that contains the data and files extracted from cloud storage)
    - **New extraction**

11. If you do not want to do any of these actions, click the **Close** button:

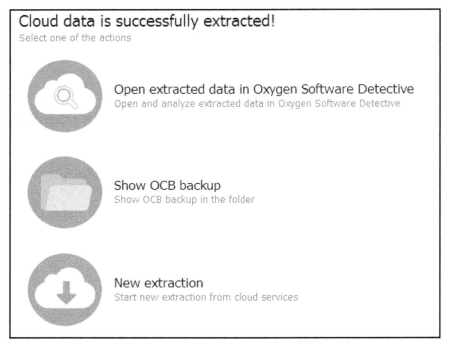

Final window of the extraction process from cloud storage

The extracted data will be available for viewing and analysis:

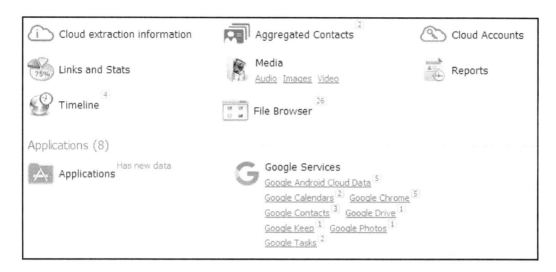

Results of the data extraction

Using Electronic Evidence Examiner to extract data from a Facebook account

Probably, there is not a single expert who has never heard of Paraben products. However, not all experts know about their functionality. The issue of Facebook account data acquisition is raised periodically at forensics forums. In this recipe, we will describe how to do it using Electronic Evidence Examiner.

Getting ready

Download **Electronic Evidence Examiner (E3: Universal)** from your personal account and activate it with an electronic license, or connect your Paraben hardware key to your computer. Following are the web pages of the E3 Universal:

- Web page of E3: Universal: `https://www.paraben.com/products/e3-universal`
- Web page of the trial version of E3: Universal: `https://www.paraben.com/forms/request-trial`

How to do it...

1. Double-click the E3: Universal icon. When the program starts, create a new case. Click the **Cloud Import** icon on the toolbar:

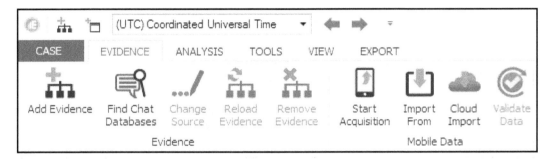

E3: Universal toolbar

2. Using this tool, you can extract data from the following cloud services: Facebook, Google Locations, Google Mail, Google Drive, and Twitter. In the open of **Cloud Data Import Wizard** window, select the **Facebook** checkbox under **Data Source** and enter the login and password from the account in the corresponding windows:

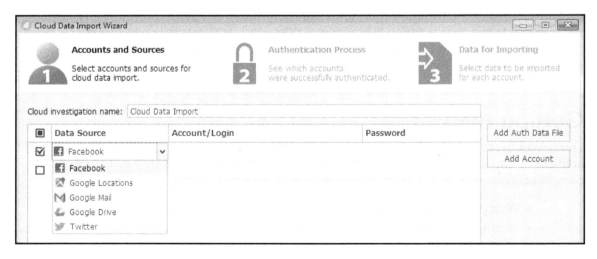

Cloud Data Import Wizard window

3. Click the **Authenticate** button. The program will check that the account data is correct and inform you about it:

The result of account data verification

4. Select the date range for which you want to extract the data and tick the types of data. Click the **Import Data** button:

Extraction options selection window

5. The process of data extraction will start. The progress will be displayed in the **Cloud Data Import Wizard** window. When the extraction is complete, click the **Finish** button. The **Task Status Notification** window will be displayed. This window contains information about the path where the data is located. Click **OK**. Then you can view and process the extracted data in E3: Universal:

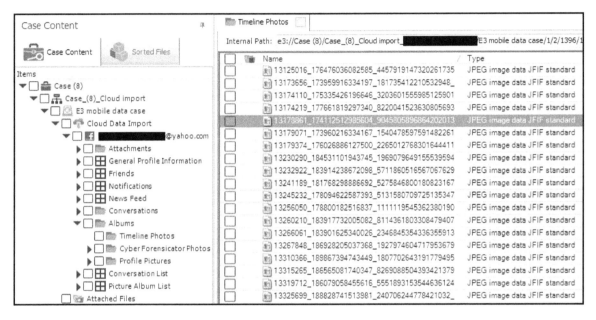

Extracted data displayed in the E3: Universal window

Using Elcomsoft Phone Breaker to extract data from iCloud

Elcomsoft Phone Breaker is the perfect tool to extract data from cloud services. Despite its modest interface, it has great functionality and extracts the maximum amount of data. The peculiarity of Elcomsoft Phone Breaker is that an expert will need additional software from the same company to view the extracted data (Elcomsoft Phone Viewer), unlike other programs described in this chapter. Elcomsoft Phone Breaker is the cheapest of all the programs we have explored for cloud services data extraction. In this recipe, we will cover the extraction of iTunes backups saved in iCloud using Elcomsoft Phone Breaker.

Getting ready

Download the program from the following links and activate it with the code that will be sent to you via email:

- The Elcomsoft Phone Breaker page is at `https://www.elcomsoft.com/eppb.html`
- The Elcomsoft Phone Viewer page is at `https://www.elcomsoft.com/epv.html`

How to do it...

1. Double-click the icon of the program to start it:

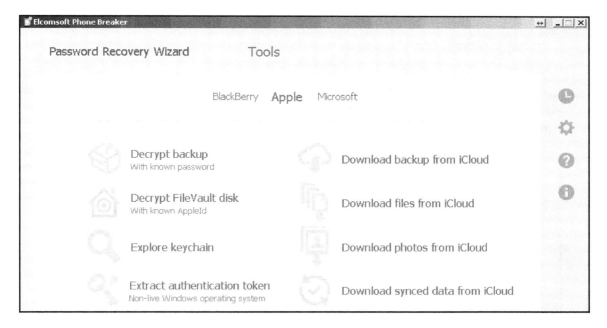

Elcomsoft Phone Breaker main window

2. Click the **Download backup from iCloud** option. In the next window, you will be prompted to select the method of authentication, by login and password or by token:

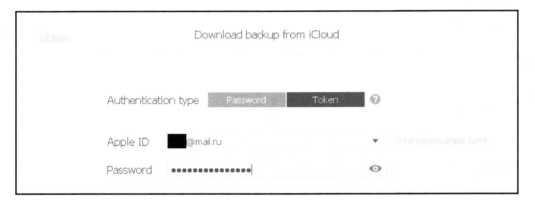

Selection of the authentication method

3. For the extraction, the examiner should have the credentials of the account. There are a lot of ways to get them. For example, the examiner can ask the owner of the account for them. Enter the credentials and click on the **Sign in** button. During the process of user identification, if the iCloud account has two-factor authentication enabled, the additional window will appear in the program, which will prompt you to enter the code sent to the trusted device.

4. Then, the backup copies of iTunes, which are in the iCloud service, will be displayed in the program window:

Backups saved in iCloud

5. Tick the iTunes backups you need and click the **Download** button. At the end of the extraction, the final window with information about the extraction will appear. You can click **Finish** to complete the extraction process, or you can click **Open in EPV** to view the data extracted from iCloud in the Elcomsoft Phone Viewer:

Window with information about data extracted from iCloud

There's more...

Using Elcomsoft Phone Breaker, you can extract data from Microsoft cloud services. For more information, read the article *Fetching Call Logs, Browsing History and Location Data from Microsoft Accounts* by *Oleg Afonin*: https://blog.elcomsoft.com/2017/06/fetching-call-logs-browsing-history-and-location-data-from-microsoft-accounts/.

Using Belkasoft Evidence Center to extract data from iCloud

Belkasoft Evidence Center was described in Chapter 2, *Android Devices Acquisition*. Now this program has a function to extract data from cloud storage. In this recipe, we will describe how to extract data from iCloud using Belkasoft Evidence Center.

How to do it...

1. Double-click the Belkasoft Evidence Center icon. When the program starts, click the **New Case** button. In the window, enter information about the new case and click **Create and open**. In the **Add data source** window, specify the path where the extracted data will be saved and click the **Cloud** button:

The Add data source window

2. In the next window, click the **iCloud** icon and then click the **Next** button:

Selecting the cloud service

3. In the next window, select the authentication method: using login and password or using the cookies of `icloud.com`. Select **Authentication using login and password**. Enter the credentials. Click the **Next** button. In the next window, select the data types that you need to extract from iCloud. Click the **Next** button:

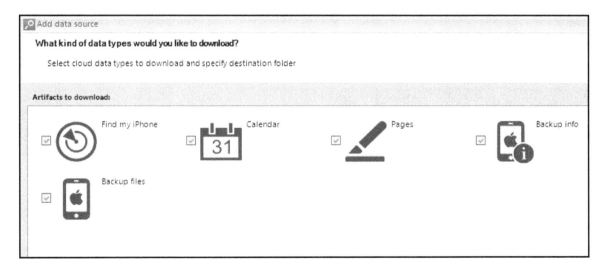

Selecting the data types saved in iCloud

4. The data extraction process will start, the progress of which will be displayed in the window of the program. When the extraction is complete, summary information about the extraction will be displayed. Click **Finish** to complete the work of the extractor.

6
SQLite Forensics

In this chapter, we'll cover the following recipes:

- Parsing SQLite databases with Belkasoft Evidence Center
- Parsing SQLite databases with DB Browser for SQLite
- Parsing SQLite databases with Oxygen Forensic SQLite Viewer
- Parsing SQLite databases with SQLite Wizard

Introduction

SQLite databases are widely used for different applications' data storage on both mobile devices and PCs. That is why analysis of such databases is highly important. According to our experience, in-depth analysis of SQLite databases allows us to extract up to 50% of additional data. This is explained in the following points:

- There are millions of applications that store their data in SQLite databases. None of the mobile forensic software developers are able to provide the support for the analysis of such a large number of applications.
- In the case of the name of the database or the path, where it is stored changes during the process of application version changing. Mobile forensic tools will not be able to recognize and analyze the database correctly.
- Not all forensic tools have an option for the automatic analysis of SQLite databases. For example, some tools extract data from Skype Freelists and some do not. The manual in-depth analysis of databases allows the extraction of their data more fully.

There are thousands of SQLite Viewers. Which tool should be chosen for analysis? According to our experience, the most efficient tools for mobile application SQLite database analysis are the tools produced by mobile forensic software developers.

Many beginning experts are afraid that they will have to deal with SQL command writing during manual SQLite database analysis. However, all advanced SQLite Viewers for database analysis use templates and visualizations of SQL commands that make databases analysis easier.

SQLite databases are generally stored in the userdata partition of the Android device.

Parsing SQLite databases with Belkasoft Evidence Center

The Belkasoft Evidence Center program has already been described previously in Chapter 2, *Android Devices Acquisition*. This program has the functionality for SQLite database analysis on both mobile devices and PCs. In this chapter, we will describe how to analyze a SQLite database with Belkasoft Evidence Center.

How to do it...

In this recipe, we will describe an interesting case. The problem was the following: on the screen of an examined iPhone 5 there was correspondence with two people on Skype, but it was not seen in the results of the analysis, the extracted data, which was displayed in the forensic tools. Before I was asked for assistance, my colleagues vainly tried all mobile forensics tools they had. The tools could not provide access to the correspondence.

The iTunes backup of this device was analyzed via Belkasoft Evidence Center (the process of it will be described in Chapter 9, *iOS Forensics*, in the *iOS backups parsing with Belkasoft Evidence Center* section) and we got the following results:

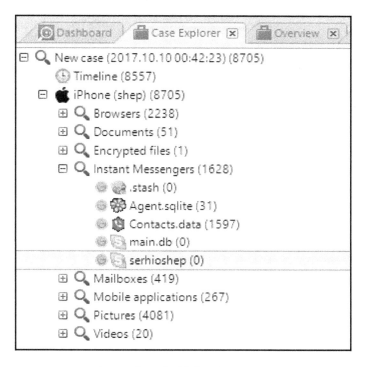

Summary of the results of the iTunes backup analysis

As can be seen from the results, there are two Skype SQLite databases in the examined iTunes backup, but no messages were found.

These databases were located in the following paths:

- Profile
  path: `image:\1\vol_0\HomeDomain\Library\com.apple.internal.ck\main.db`
- Profile path: `image:\1\vol_0\AppDomain-com.skype.skype\Library\Application Support\Skype4LifeSlimCore\serhioshep\main.db`

As an example of SQLite database analysis, we will deal with the `main.db` file, which is located in the `serhioshep` folder:

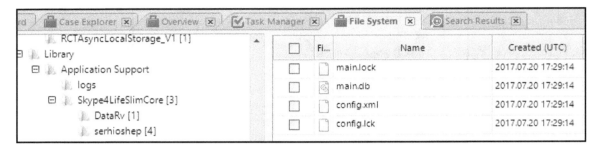

main.db file

Double-click the **File System** tab and go to the file:

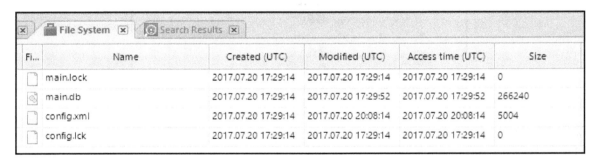

main.db file

As can be seen in the following figure, the size of the `main.db` file is 266 KB, meaning that it may contain the correspondence we are looking for.

Double-click the `main.db` file and select the **Sqlite** tab in the lower window. In this window, the categories of the data contained in the examined database will be displayed. For example, in the **Accounts** category, we can see the `serhioshep` record. It is a Skype name of an account:

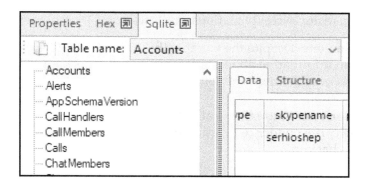

Categories of the main.db file.

However, there is no information in the **Messages** category. If you click on the **Hex** tab of this window, you can see that there is no data in this part of the examined database:

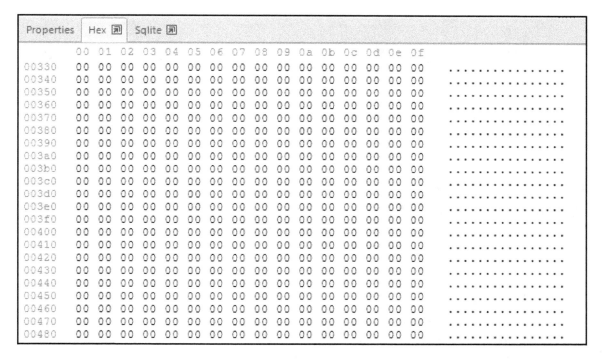

Data contained in the main.db file in Hex mode

Similar result were received when we examined the second `main.db` file.

What happened? There are two explanations:

- **Explanation one**: Despite the fact that these files are SQLite databases, they do not contain information about messages. Perhaps this happened because the device's security settings did not allow this information to be transferred to the iTunes backup.
- **Explanation two**: These files really do not contain correspondence and the device shows the correspondence saved in the WAL-file, which was not transferred to the iTunes backup.

The solution is that we need to jailbreak the device. Jailbreaking can give us full access to the file system of the device so we can extract more data from the device. The `main.db` files will be available for analysis in unchanged form, and also the WAL-files will be available if they are present in the device's memory. This method will help us to extract the Skype correspondence.

Parsing SQLite databases with DB Browser for SQLite

DB Browser for SQLite is a free tool that can be used for SQLite database analysis. It has great functionalities for such data analysis.

Getting ready

Open the DB Browser for the SQLite program website in your browser. Select the version of the program that is suitable for your operating system and download it. Double-click the icon of the downloaded file and follow the instructions to install it.

How to do it...

Double-click the icon of the DB Browser for the SQLite program; it will start the program. You can create your SQLite database or analyze the one that already exists. In this chapter, we will describe how to analyze the contents of the `mmssms.db` file.

Click **Open Database**. Select the file, which you will examine. Click **OK**:

Toolbar of the DB Browser for SQLite

The examined file will be uploaded in the program. The main window of the program has four tabs:

1. **Database Structure**: Displays the structure of the database.
2. **Browse Data**: Displays the data contained in the database.
3. **EditPramas**: Parameters of the database analysis.
4. **Execute SQL**: GUI interface in which you can provide SQL commands.

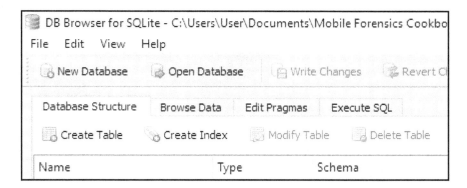

Tabs of the main window of the program

In the **Database Structure** tab, the database structure that was uploaded is displayed. In this case, the examined database contains two tables, android_metadata and sms:

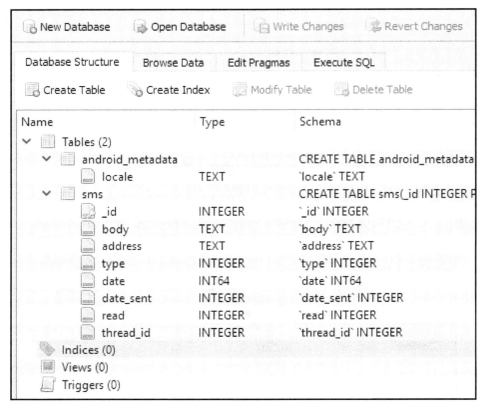

Structure of the examined database

Go to the **Browse Data** tab and select the sms table from the drop-down menu. In the main window of the program, a table will be displayed showing the sequence number of a record, the SMS text, the phone number, type (incoming SMS or outgoing), date, sending date, status (if the SMS message is read or not), and so on:

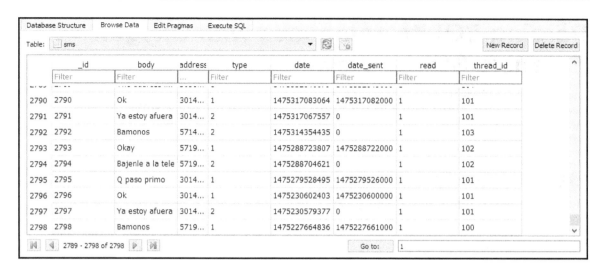

	_id	body	address	type	date	date_sent	read	thread_id
	Filter	Filter	...	Filter	Filter	Filter	Filter	Filter
2790	2790	Ok	3014...	1	1475317083064	1475317082000	1	101
2791	2791	Ya estoy afuera	3014...	2	1475317067557	0	1	101
2792	2792	Bamonos	5714...	2	1475314354435	0	1	103
2793	2793	Okay	5719...	1	1475288723807	1475288722000	1	102
2794	2794	Bajenle a la tele	5719...	2	1475288704621	0	1	102
2795	2795	Q paso primo	3014...	1	1475279528495	1475279526000	1	101
2796	2796	Ok	3014...	1	1475230602403	1475230600000	1	101
2797	2797	Ya estoy afuera	3014...	2	1475230579377	0	1	101
2798	2798	Bamonos	5719...	1	1475227664836	1475227661000	1	100

Data contained in the sms table

As can be seen in the figure, it is not clear what format the values in the `date` and `date_sent` columns are specified in. Interpretation of these values can cause difficulties for an inexperienced expert. Also, remember the number of records in this table (2,798), as it will be important for us when we describe Oxygen Forensic SQLite Viewer.

There's more...

Besides the SQLite databases, data may be contained in the WAL-files. WAL files are Write Ahead Logs. They contain some pages from a SQLite database. You should also analyze available WAL-files if you want to extract maximum data from a mobile device.

See also

- DB Browser for the SQLite website: `http://sqlitebrowser.org/`
- The website of another free tool for SQLite databases analysis, Sqliteman: `https://sourceforge.net/projects/sqliteman/`
- The program for WAL-files analysis, Walitean: `https://github.com/n0fate/walitean`

Parsing SQLite databases with Oxygen Forensic SQLite Viewer

The Oxygen Forensic program has been already described previously in Chapter 1, *SIM Cards Acquisition and Analysis*. This program has an Oxygen Forensic SQLite Viewer module, which can be used for SQLite database viewing and analysis.

Getting ready

Oxygen Forensic SQLite Viewer can be started by completing three steps:

1. Double-click the OxySQLiteViewer64.exe file, which is located at the following path: 'C:\Program Files (x86)\Oxygen Software\Oxygen Forensic Detective'.

2. Double-click the Oxygen Forensic program icon. In the toolbar of the program, select **Tools** and then **SQLite Database Viewer**:

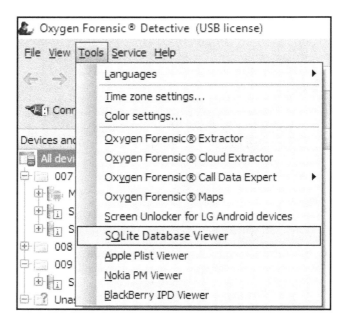

Tools menu

3. In the main **Case** window, click the **File Browser** section. In the opened window of the section, select the **Database files** tab. In this window, all the databases including deleted ones will be displayed. Select the database you want to examine. Left click on it. In the drop-down window select **Open in SQLite Viewer**.

How to do it...

Double-click the file of the `OxySQLiteViewer64.exe` program, which is located in the `C:\Program Files (x86)\Oxygen Software\Oxygen Forensic Detective` path. In the toolbar of the program, select **File** and then **Open**. Select the file you want to examine and click **OK**. In order to compare the functionality of the programs, we will describe the analysis of the same `mmssms.db` file.

The window of the program is divided into three areas:

- **Area 1**: **Tables** bar-In this bar, the structure of SQLite database files, which are uploaded to the program, is displayed.

Structure of the mmssms.db file

As can be seen in the screenshot, besides 2,798 records that the database contains, the program managed to restore 13 more records.

- **Area 2**: The main working area of the program where the data is displayed:

#		_id	body	address	type	date	date_sent	read	thread_id	Offset
2787	☑	2787	Para q tanta …	30144…	1	1475360185783	1475360185000	1	101	
2788	☑	2788	Eso primo	30144…	1	1475360033511	1475360032000	1	101	
2789	☑	2789	The address i…	30388…	1	1475332846679	1475332845000	1	104	
2790	☑	2790	Ok	30144…	1	1475317083064	1475317082000	1	101	
2791	☑	2791	Ya estoy afu…	30144…	2	1475317067557	0	1	101	
2792	☑	2792	Bamonos	57146…	2	1475314354435	0	1	103	
2793	☑	2793	Okay	57199…	1	1475288723807	1475288722000	1	102	
2794	☑	2794	Bajenle a la t…	57199…	2	1475288704621	0	1	102	
2795	☑	2795	Q paso primo	30144…	1	1475279528495	1475279526000	1	101	
2796	☑	2796	Ok	30144…	1	1475230602403	1475230600000	1	101	
2797	☑	2797	Ya estoy afu…	30144…	2	1475230579377	0	1	101	
2798	☑	2798	Bamonos	57199…	1	1475227664836	1475227661000	1	100	
2799	☑ 🗑	72	Se la pelo pa…	57122…	1	1500654080655	1500654078000	1	133	00012547
2800	☑ 🗑	61	Dise la senor…	70358…	2	1500756236783	0	1	260	00013047
2801	☑ 🗑	59	Pero esta vie…	70358…	1	1500766900530	1500766900000	1	260	00013225
2802	☑ 🗑	55	Me puedes c…	+1323…	2	1500825632415	0	1	149	00013434
2803	☑ 🗑	49	Deje la nina c…	32327…	2	1500826882133	0	1	99	00013686
2804	☑ 🗑	45	Estan las luze…	57136…	2	1500856958045	0	1	117	00013884
2805	☑ 🗑		Can you plea…	ody ov…	1	11154199730…	35684339753…	1	105	00014001
2806	☑ 🗑	37	Manana vam…	70394…	2	1501118575710	0	1	116	00014471
2807	☑ 🗑	29	Manana teba…	57124…	1	1501208231832	1501208231000	1	200	00014865
2808	☑ 🗑	28	Levantas al g…	57124…	1	1501208278636	1501208278000	1	200	00014932
2809	☑ 🗑	19	Son 2 dias. u…	57124…	2	1501292955840	0	1	200	00015414
2810	☑ 🗑	12	Todavia no v…	32327…	2	1501347654310	0	1	99	00015801

View of the main working window of the Oxygen Forensic SQLite Viewer program

As can be seen in the screenshot, new additional records appeared in the table, and if you click the **Blocks containing deleted data** tab, you will see that these blocks contain text, which was probably transferred there from SMS messages that the program did not manage to restore:

A fragment of the SMS message contained in the Blocks containing deleted data tab

The main window of the program also contains the following tabs:

Table structure: Shows the structure of the analyzed SQLite database

SQL Editor and **Visual Query Builder**: Allow you to specify SQL commands to analyze similar databases

- **Area 3**: The bar, which is located on the right, automatically converts the value of a cell using several algorithms. It is very convenient to use for converting the examined database's cells values:

Type	Value
UTF-8	1475288723807
Unicode (UTF-16 BE)	ㄴ嬈徴帞俶謽
Unicode (UTF-16 LE)	㕘
OLE Automation Date	25.09.1465 1085:04:09
Unix Epoch Time	15.01.48720 23:16:47
Unix Epoch Time (ms)	01.10.2016 2:25:23
Unix Epoch Time (micro)	18.01.1970 1:48:08
OS X Epoch Time	15.01.48751 23:16:47
BlackBerry Time	<Can't convert>
Chrome Time	18.01.1601 1:48:08
Symbian Epoch Time	<Can't convert>
MS File Time	02.01.1601 16:58:49
Unsigned-8	<Can't convert>
Signed-8	<Can't convert>
Unsigned-16	<Can't convert>
Signed-16	<Can't convert>
Unsigned-32	<Can't convert>
Signed-32	<Can't convert>
Signed-64	1475288723807
Single	<Can't convert>
Double	1475288723807
Uuencoded	EEOI?□I6□
Base64	ЧЋщЫП;Ы□4
Base64 (UTF8)	□弑□□4
Base64 (UTF-16 LE)	軗□槩傐
Base64 (UTF-16 BE)	힗丰렜□

The appearance of the left panel

As can be seen in the figure, the value of the `date` cells in the examined database are stores in the Unix Epoch Time (ms) format. The value, contained in the examined cell, is `01.10.2016 2:25:23`.

There's more...

Summing up what was said earlier, we can say that with the use of specialized SQLite databases editors, experts extract not only more data by restoring deleted records, but they also restore fragments from other areas of databases that may be interesting to them. Using SQL Editor and Visual Query Builder, you can write scripts that will automatize in-depth analysis of such databases.

Parsing SQLite databases with SQLite Wizard

The UFED program has already been described previously in `Chapter 4`, *Windows Phones and BlackBerry Acquisition*. This program has the SQLite Wizard module, which can be used for data extraction from SQLite databases.

Getting ready

Unfortunately, the SQLite Wizard module cannot be started individually, and before using it, an expert has to analyze extracted data from a mobile device via UFED Physical Analyzer. When the analysis is done, click the category:

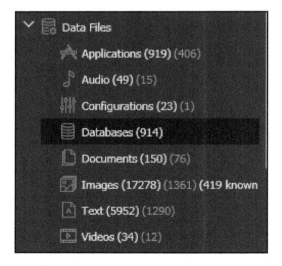

Databases category

In the main window of the program, the tab will be displayed that contains information about SQLite databases extracted from the examined mobile device. The window will also display information on whether the database was analyzed via UFED Physical Analyzer or not:

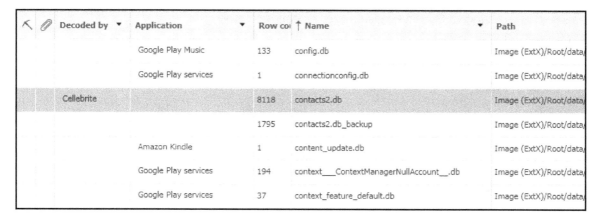

	Decoded by ▾	Application ▾	Row co ↑	Name	▾	Path
		Google Play Music	133	config.db		Image (ExtX)/Root/data/
		Google Play services	1	connectionconfig.db		Image (ExtX)/Root/data/
	Cellebrite		8118	contacts2.db		Image (ExtX)/Root/data/
			1795	contacts2.db_backup		Image (ExtX)/Root/data/
		Amazon Kindle	1	content_update.db		Image (ExtX)/Root/data/
		Google Play services	194	context___ContextManagerNullAccount__.db		Image (ExtX)/Root/data/
		Google Play services	37	context_feature_default.db		Image (ExtX)/Root/data/

Information about databases displayed in the main window of UFED Physical Analyzer

Viewing this window, an expert will face an unpleasant discovery. It turns out that most of the extracted SQLite databases cannot be analyzed, meaning that some of the data, sometimes very important data, can be lost.

How to do it...

As an example, we will describe the analysis of the `contacts2.db_backup` database. In the main window of the UFED Physical Analyzer program, click the right mouse button on the file. In the drop-down menu, select **SQLite Wizard**. The opened window will prompt you to fill in the **Application** and **Name** fields. Fill them in and click **Next**.

In the next window, the **Query builder** tab will be opened, in which the structures of the tables that are included in the examined file will be displayed. Add them to the desktop of the program by double-clicking on them. On the desktop, you can specify how the tables should be related. As the structure of the examined database is known, there is no need to make additional manipulations. Click the **Next** button.

SQLite Wizard contains a great number of templates that make an expert's work much easier. Click on the drop-down menu and select the **Contacts** template:

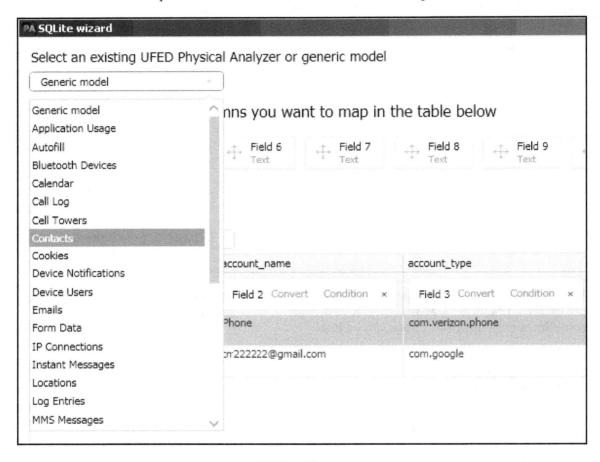

SQLite WizardR17 templates

In the upper part of the window, there will be rectangles, which will display the categories of the **Contacts** database; the table containing the values will be presented below. Drag the rectangles with the categories to the columns that correspond to them. It is fine if some rectangles with categories remain unused. Click the **Next** button.

In the new window, you can specify the settings: whether to use the newly generated SQLite database analysis scheme for this analysis, or whether to use this analysis scheme for all subsequent examinations of mobile devices.

You can close the SQLite Wizard by clicking the **Close** button, or run the analysis using the new `contacts2.db_backup` database analysis algorithm by clicking the **Run** button. At the end of the analysis, the extracted data will be added to what was received earlier.

See also

- *Mobile forensics: UFED vs Magnet Acquire,* `https://www.digitalforensics.com/blog/mobile-forensics-ufed-vs-magnet-acquire/`

7
Understanding Plist Forensics

In this chapter, we'll cover the following recipes:

- Parsing plist with Apple Plist Viewer
- Parsing plist with Belkasoft Evidence Center
- Parsing plist with plist Editor Pro
- Parsing plist with Plist Explorer

Introduction

Property lists (**plist**) are system files that are used in the iOS and macOS operating systems for different kinds of data storage. They can be used by both operating systems and applications. Plists are good for storing arrays, dictionaries, and strings.

Plists are XML files, but with some differences. For example, the order of tags in this file is determined by some rules: they are key-value pairs, but tags of the `key` type and tags of the `value` type are on the same level. For example:

```
<key>Device Name</key>
<string>iPhone Olja</string>
<key>GUID</key>
<string>D526CA3328B0A964372B4E93C12D5C74</string>
<key>ICCID</key>
<string>897010220192766690f</string>
<key>IMEI</key>
<string>013429003240443</string>
```

In order to speed up the process of reading and writing, `plist` are often made binary by converting them into **binary plist (bplist)** format. An expert has to decode this kind of file by using a special tool to extract the data contained in it.

As a rule, experts examine iOS backups received from various mobile devices, such as iPods, iPads, and iPhones. These backups contain a large number of plist-files.

 You can read about some of the most common plist-files contained in iTunes backups in the book *Practical Mobile Forensics, Second Edition* by *Heather Mahalik* and *Rohit Tamma*.

Each iOS backup, along with the backup data file, contains four metafiles: `Info.plist`, `Manifest.plist`, `Status.plist`, and `Manifest.mbdb`.

Let's have a look at each of these metafiles:

- `Info.plist`: This is a configuration file that contains information about the device, product type, product version, IMEI, phone number, date of the last backup, serial number, synchronization settings, list of applications installed on the device, and so on.
- `Manifest.plist`: This is a configuration file that contains additional information about third-party applications, the backup keybag, the password protection flag (`WasPasscodeSet`), the backup encryption flag (`IsEncrypted`), and so on.

- `Status.plist`: This is a configuration file that contains information about the backup: the backup status, the full backup flag (`IsFullBackup`), the backup date, and the backup version.
- `Manifest.mbdb` This is a binary file that contains information about all other files in the backup, including the file size and information about the filesystem structure.

fd0f81badaf05fc662693db39fd8cc710a4e61f9	12/5/2012 4:34 PM	File	179 KB
fdda2f81cc0b838dc00e3050b14da7ef2d835f3c	7/10/2013 11:47 AM	File	260 KB
fdfe12593b966c26c0db4b9847a7103cb9a2a...	7/10/2013 11:47 AM	File	5 KB
fef90f6717898f8cdcd49ed1a40f0bc90a229814	12/5/2012 4:34 PM	File	1 KB
Info.plist	7/10/2013 11:47 AM	PLIST File	29 KB
Manifest.mbdb	7/10/2013 11:47 AM	MBDB File	140 KB
Manifest.plist	7/10/2013 11:47 AM	PLIST File	7 KB
Status.plist	7/10/2013 11:47 AM	PLIST File	1 KB

iTunes backup metafiles

Parsing plist with Apple Plist Viewer

The Oxygen Forensic program has been already described previously in `Chapter 1`, *SIM Cards Acquisition and Analysis*. This program contains the Apple Plist Viewer module, which can be used for viewing and analyzing the contents of a plist-file.

How to do it...

1. Double-click the Oxygen Forensic icon to start. In the program menu, select **Tools** and then **Apple Plist Viewer**:

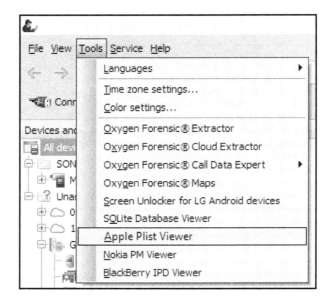

Apple Plist Viewer startup

2. The Windows window will appear; you need to select the plist-file which will be analyzed. In this example, the `History.plist` file was analyzed. After file selection, click **Open**.

3. After that, the main window of the Apple Plist Viewer opens, where the result of the selected plist-file will be displayed:

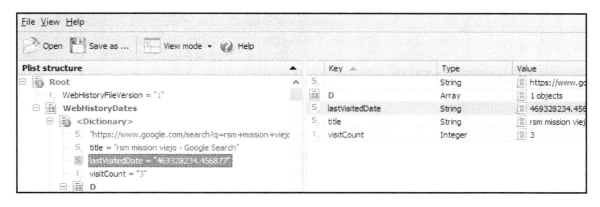

Displaying the analysis result of the plist-file in Classic mode

The viewing of the results is possible in two modes, **Classic mode** and **Simple mode**:

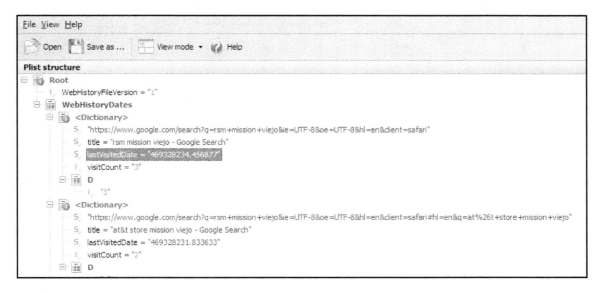

Displaying the analysis result of the plist-file in Simple mode

4. Switching between the modes can be done by clicking the **View mode** button that is located on the toolbar of the program.

5. There is a secondary window on the right-hand side of the program. If, in the window where the results of analysis are displayed, the selected value is a time value, then in the secondary window the decoding results of the time will be displayed in different formats:

Type	Value
UTF-8	469328234.456...
Unicode (UTF-16...	伅恬涝粬褒仟...
Unicode (UTF-16...	坐外吒孫口匪...
OLE Automation ...	20.01.41693 10...
Unix Epoch Time	15.11.1984 0:5...
Unix Epoch Time...	06.01.1970 10:...
Unix Epoch Time...	01.01.1970 0:0...
OS X Epoch Time	16.11.2015 0:5...

Decoding results of the time value, displayed in different formats

Parsing plist with Belkasoft Evidence Center

The Belkasoft Evidence Center program has already been described previously in Chapter 2, *Android Devices Acquisition*. This program has the functionality for analyzing the plist-files of mobile devices. In this chapter, we will describe how to analyze plist-files via Belkasoft Evidence Center.

How to do it...

1. Double-click on the Belkasoft Evidence Center icon. When the program starts, click **New Case**. In the opened window, enter the data for the new case, specify the path where the case files will be saved, and click the **Create and open** button.

2. Since in the Belkasoft Evidence Center program there is no option to select a separate file for analysis, you must specify the folder that contains one or more plist-file as a data source.

3. In the new **Add data source** window, specify the path to the plist-files that you want to analyze and click the **Next** button:

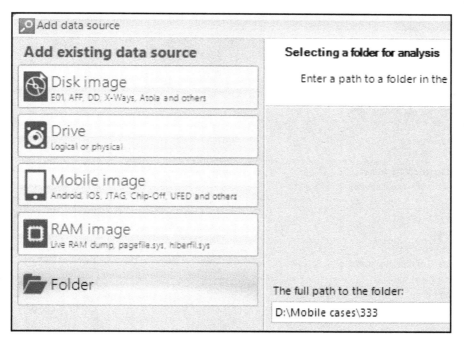

Add data source window

4. In the next window, select the artifacts categories that are relevant to the iOS operating system. Click the **Finish** button:

iOS artifacts selection

5. After processing the folder with the plist-files, the results of the preliminary analysis can be viewed in the **Overview** tab. If the examined file is known to the program, then its data will be displayed in a handy form:

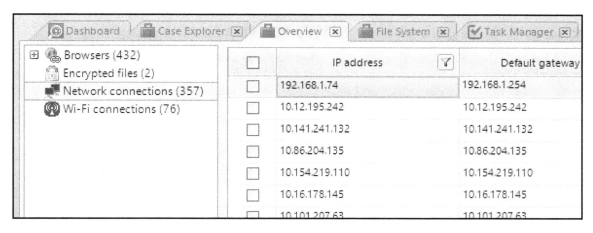

The Overview tab of Belkasoft Evidence Center

6. If you want to view the contents of a particular plist-file, go to the **File System** tab and specify the file you need. In the window where the file contents are displayed, on the toolbar, select **Plist**. In this window, you can manually view the examined file contents:

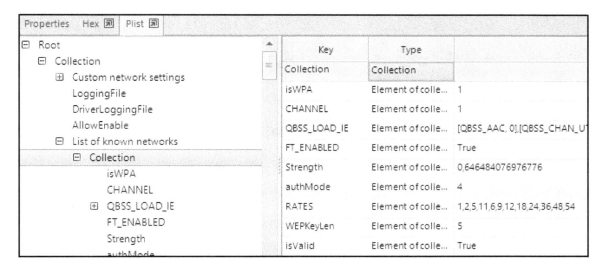

Contents of the com.apple.wifi.plist-file

Parsing plist with plist Editor Pro

Plist Editor Pro is a tool for plist-files analysis that was recommended by *Heather Mahalik* and *Rohit Tamma*, the authors of the book *Practical Mobile Forensics, Second Edition.* Using this tool, plist-files with XML format and binary files can be analyzed.

Getting ready

Download the tool to your computer and install it, following the instructions from the installer.

The plist Editor Pro web page can be found at `http://www.icopybot.com/plist-editor.htm`.

How to do it...

1. Start the program by double-clicking on the icon:

Plist Editor Pro icon

2. When the program starts, select **View** and then **Read only mode** in the menu. It will protect the examined file contents from accidental changes:

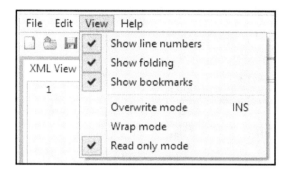

The Read only mode flag in the View menu

3. In order to open the plist-file, in the drop-down **File** menu, select **Open**:

```
XML View │ List View
    1       <?xml version="1.0" encoding="UTF-8"?>
    2       <!DOCTYPE plist PUBLIC "-//Apple//DTD PLIST 1.0//EN" "http://www.apple.com,
    3       <plist version="1.0">
    4       <dict>
    5          <key>Custom network settings</key>
    6          <dict>
    7             <key>The Elms</key>
    8             <string>27E31195-7337-43C2-B5C2-8BA0B62AA191</string>
    9             <key>kathryn</key>
   10             <string>F60DAFC8-ED23-41E1-AC04-E091F47B3DAE</string>
   11             <key>Marriott_CONF</key>
   12             <string>5BA3199E-E849-4000-8CFB-C8EE5749C65C</string>
   13             <key>VerizonWiFiAccess</key>
   14             <string>5EC92D7D-455F-49BB-A7F5-4BD090BCFE43</string>
   15          </dict>
   16          <key>LoggingFile</key>
   17          <string>/Library/Logs/wifi.log</string>
   18          <key>DriverLoggingFile</key>
   19          <string>/Library/Logs/wifi_driver.log</string>
   20          <key>AllowEnable</key>
   21          <integer>1</integer>
```

XML View mode

---

[177]

In the opened window, select the file and click **Open**. The opened file can be viewed in two modes, **XML View** and **List View**:

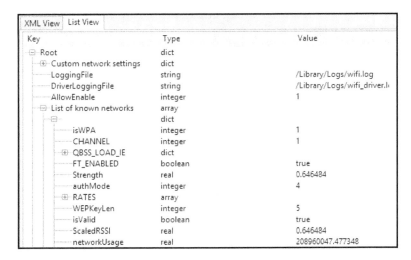

List View mode

Parsing plist with Plist Explorer

Plist Explorer is a free tool developed by the Dec Software company.

Getting ready

Download the program and unpack the archive. The program does not require installation on your computer.

How to do it...

1. Double-click the icon of the program:

Plist Explorer icon

2. The main window of the Plist Explorer program is divided into three sections. Using the first section, you can specify partition and folder where the examined plist-file is located. Using the second section, you can specify the examined file.

3. In the second section, when you specify the file which is to be examined, its contents will be shown in the third section. The contents of the examined file will be shown in hexadecimal notation at the bottom of the third section:

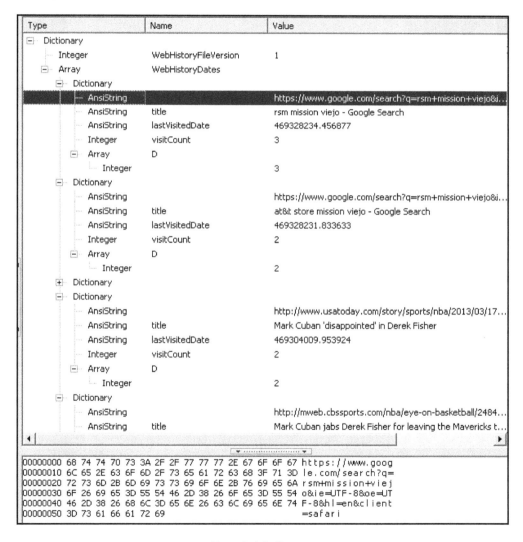

The examined plist-file contents

There's more...

The program download page is located
at www.ithmbconverter.com/plist/plistexplorer.zip.

A discussion of the program can be found at the following page: http://www.
forensicfocus.com/Forums/viewtopic/t=8635/.

8
Analyzing Physical Dumps and Backups of Android Devices

In this chapter, we'll cover the following recipes:

- Android physical dumps and backups parsing with Autopsy
- Android TOT container parsing with Oxygen Forensics
- Android backups parsing with Belkasoft Evidence Center
- Android physical dumps and backups parsing with AXIOM
- Android physical dumps parsing with Encase Forensic
- Thumbnails analysis with ThumbnailExpert

Introduction

There are a lot of tools for analysis of physical dumps and backups of mobile devices running Android operating systems. These tools include all the best mobile forensics tools, such as UFED Physical Analyzer (Cellebrite), Oxygen Forensics (Oxygen Forensics, Inc), .XRY (MSAB), MOBILedit Forensic Express (COMPELSON Labs), and Secure View (Susteen).

Computer forensics software developers also try to include the functionality for extracting and analyzing mobile devices in their products. These tools are: Encase Forensic (OpenText Corp.), MPE+ (AccessData), Belkasoft Evidence Center (Belkasoft), AXIOM (Magnet Forensics), E3: UNIVERSAL (Paraben Corporation), and so on.

It is surprising, but some mobile forensics experts do not know that physical dumps and backups can be analyzed via a free tool – Autopsy, or via a cheap tool that has good functionality - Andriller.

Manufacturers of hardware solutions for damaged mobile device analysis, such as Rusolut Sp. and ACE Lab companies, also include in their products (Visual NAND Reconstructor (Rusolut Sp.) and PC-3000 MOBILE (ACE Lab)), the functionality for deleted data restoring and SQLite databases analysis.

Unfortunately, the volume of this chapter does not give us an opportunity to discuss all of these nice programs. In this chapter, we will cover only some of them.

Android physical dumps and backups parsing with Autopsy

The undeniable advantage of Autopsy over other mobile forensics tools is that it is free, meaning that it is available for anyone who wants to analyze his mobile device. Physical dumps of mobile devices running Android operating systems can be analyzed via Autopsy.

Getting ready

Go to the website of the program. In the website's menu select **Autopsy | Download** and click **Download Now**. On the download page, select the version of the program that corresponds to your operating system by clicking on **Download 64-bit** or **Download 32-bit**. When the installation file is downloaded, go to the directory on your computer where the downloaded files are saved, and double-click the icon of the downloaded file. Follow the instructions during installation of the program.

How to do it...

1. Double click on the icon of the program. In the **Welcome** window, click on the **Create New Case** icon; it will open the **New Case Information** window. Enter **Case Name** and enter **Base Directory** by clicking the **Browse** button. Click the **Next** button.

2. In the next window, fill in the **Case Number** and **Examiner** fields. Click the **Finish** button.

3. In the new **Add Data Source** window, click the **Disk Image or VM File** button and then click **Next**.

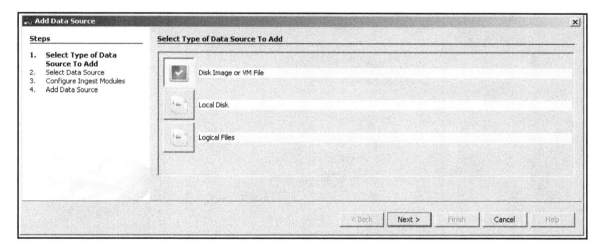

The appearance of the Add Data Source window

4. In the next window, select the physical dump of the mobile device that was created earlier (for example, with the guidelines described in Chapter 2, *Android Devices Acquisition*). Specify the time zone. Click **Next**.

5. In the next window, tick the module of the program that you need to use during the analysis. The more modules are selected, the more time it will take for the physical dump analysis. There is no need to use the **E01 Verifier** and **Virtual Machine Extractor** modules for the analysis of the mobile device's physical dump. Click the **Next** button, when the modules are selected. Click **Finish**.

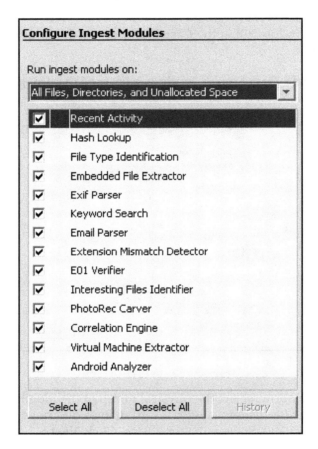

Selection of the program's modules

6. The process of selected physical dump analysis will start. The analysis progress will be displayed in the progress bar located in the lower right corner of the program's window. The data extracted from the examined physical dump will be displayed in the left part of the program during the analysis. This data can be viewed immediately, even during the process of analysis. When new data is extracted, it will be added to the relevant categories.

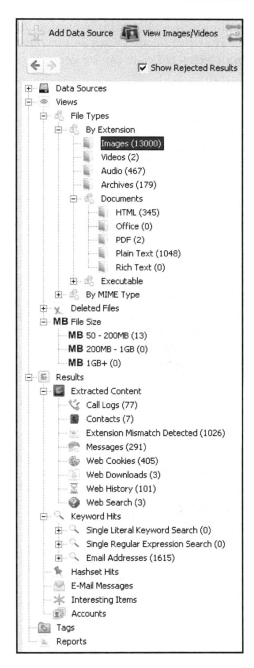

Categories of the data extracted during the physical dump analysis

As can be seen from the preceding screenshot, a large number of different data is extracted during the process of physical dump analysis. It can be viewed in the workspace of the program. Also, the report about extracted data can be generated via Autopsy.

See also

- The Autopsy download page at: `http://www.sleuthkit.org/autopsy/download.php`

Android TOT container parsing with Oxygen Forensics

The Oxygen Forensic program has already been described in the `Chapter 1`, *SIM Cards Acquisition and Analysis*. The Oxygen Forensic program has a specialized Oxygen Forensic Extractor module that can be used to make logical extraction, backup, and physical dump of a mobile device running Android operating systems. The Oxygen Forensic program is able to import and analyze the mobile device's data extracted via other hardware and software. The program can import the following types of images and data of Android devices:

- Android backup
- Android physical image
- Android YAFSS physical image
- JTAG image
- Filesystem tarball or ZIP archive
- Filesystem image folder
- Nandroid backup Nandroid (CWM)
- Nandroid Nandroid (TWRM)
- Android TOT container

As an example, the import of data from Android TOT containers will be described. These containers can be created by some types of flashers during the process of an Android device's memory reading.

How to do it...

1. Click the arrow that is located to the right of the **Import file** button on the toolbar to import data from a container. In the drop-down menu, go to **Import Android backup/image** and then **Import Android TOT container...**, as shown in the following screenshot:

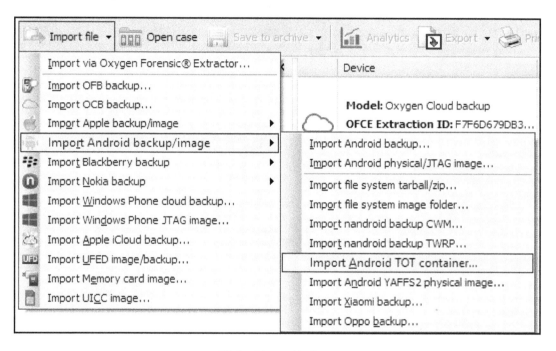

Selection of the type of data import

2. In the opened window, specify the path to the TOT file. Select it and click the **Open** button.

3. In the new window, fill in the details of the case, such as: **Device alias**, **Case number**, **Evidence number**, **Place**, **Incident number**, **Inspector**, **Device owner**, **Owner email,** and so on. If necessary, select the data that you want to restore in the **Search and recover deleted data** section. The process of data restoring will take additional time. Click the **Next** button.

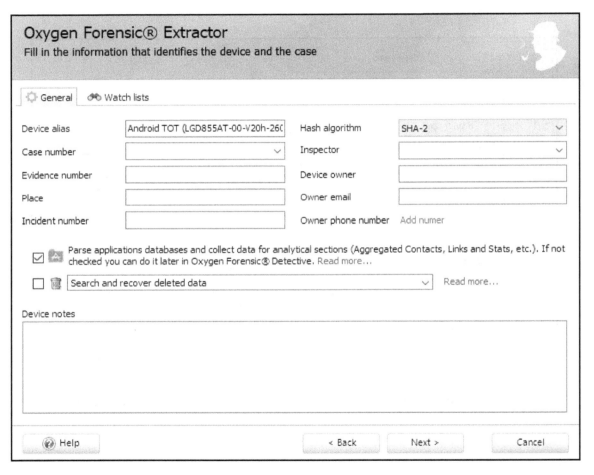

Window of Oxygen Forensic Extractor with information about the case and extraction's option

4. The program will prompt you to double-check the entered data by displaying it in the window. If all the data is correct, click the **Extract** button. The import process will start.

5. When the data import is finished, the final window of Oxygen Forensic Extractor with summary information about the import will be displayed. Click **Finish** to finish the data extraction.

6. The extracted data will be available for viewing and analysis.

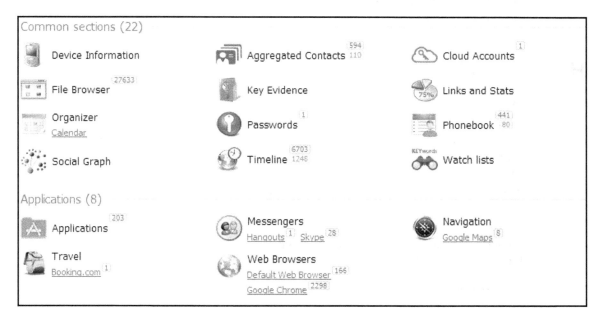

Information about extracted data in the main window of the program

Android backups parsing with Belkasoft Evidence Center

The Belkasoft Evidence Center program has already been described in `Chapter 2`, *Android Devices Acquisition*. This program has functionality for data import from physical dumps and backups of Android mobile devices.

In this chapter, we will describe how to analyze a backup of an Android mobile device via Belkasoft Evidence Center.

How to do it...

1. Double-click the icon of the program. When the program is started, create a new case. Click the **New Case** button.
2. Fill in the following fields: **Case name**, **Root folder**, **Case folder**, **Investigator**, and **Time zone**. If necessary, you can add a more detailed description of the case in the **Description** window.
3. After that, click the **Create and open** button located at the bottom of this window. In the next window, in the drop-down menu, you can select the category of files that will be displayed in it.
4. Select the **Android backup file (* .ab)** category, select the Android device's backup file, and then click the **Next** button.

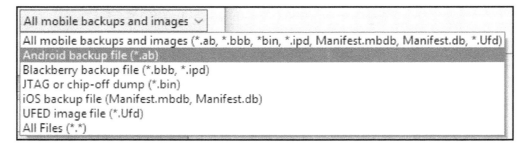

Selection of the files' category that will be displayed in the window of the program

5. After that the window will be opened. You will be prompted to select the types of artifacts you need to search for. In addition to artifacts that are directly related to Android mobile devices, you can search for documents, graphics files, and video files.

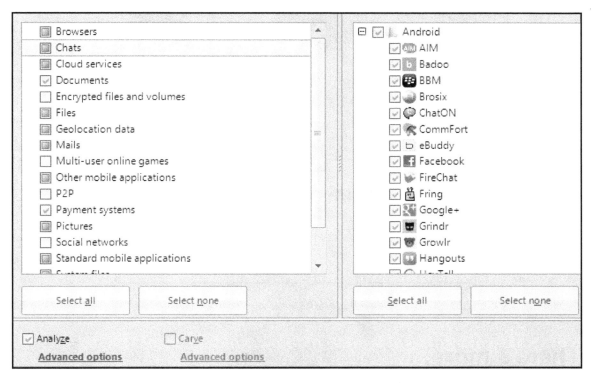

Selection of the artifacts types, the search of which has to be done

6. When you select the types of artifacts you need to search for, click the **Finish** button. The process of the Android mobile device's backup analysis will start. When the analysis is finished, you can view the extracted information and files in the **Case Explorer and Overview** tabs:

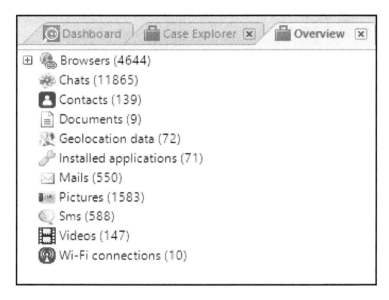

Information about extracted data displayed in the Overview tab

There's more...

The article *Extracting data from dump of mobile devices running Android operating system* can be found at: https://articles.forensicfocus.com/2014/10/28/extracting-data-from-dump-of-mobile-devices-running-android-operating-system/

Android physical dumps and backups parsing with AXIOM

The AXIOM program, developed by the Magnet Forensics company, is a popular tool that is used both for computer forensics and for mobile forensics. It has three components:

- **Magnet Acquire** is a tool designed for data acquiring from hard disks, mobile devices, and other media (this tool was described in Chapter 2, *Android Devices Acquisition*)
- **AXIOM Process** is a tool designed for analysis of devices' images, files, and folders
- **AXIOM Examine** is a tool in which the results of a performed analysis are displayed

The AXIOM program is able to extract data from Android mobile devices and analyze backups and physical dumps of such devices created earlier via Magnet Acquire or other tools.

In this chapter, we will describe the analysis of an Android mobile device via AXIOM.

Getting ready

On the website of the developer, you can request a trial version of AXIOM with the full product functionality for 30 days. You will receive an email to the email address specified during the registration. The email will contain a link for the installation file and the license activation code.

Click on the link and download the installation file. The installation file can also be downloaded from the account after registration on the website. Click on the icon of the installation file and install the program following the instructions. After installation of the program, there will be two icons, AXIOM Process and AXIOM Examine, on the desktop. Start the AXIOM Process program by double-clicking on the icon. When the program is run for the first time, the informational window will be displayed, in which you are informed that a license for the program has not been detected. To activate the license, enter the code sent to you in the email in the **License key** field. Click the **OK** button. Restart the program.

How to do it...

1. Double-click the AXIOM Process icon. In the program's window, click the **CREATE NEW CASE** button. In the next window, fill in the case information fields, such as: **Case number**, **Folder name**, **File path**, and **Scanned by.** Then click the **GO TO EVIDENCE SOURCES** button. In the next window, in the **SELECT EVIDENCE SOURCE** section, click the MOBILE icon. In the next window, click the ANDROID icon.

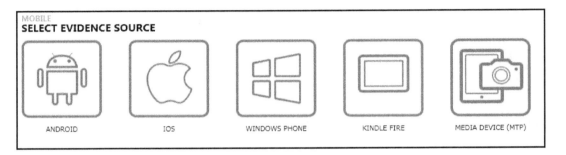

SELECT EVIDENCE SOURCE (MOBILE) section

2. In the next window, click the LOAD EVIDENCE icon. In the next window, click on the IMAGE icon. In the opened additional **Select the image** window, select the Android device backup file that you want to examine and click on the **Open** button. Analysis of the file will take some time, after which, you will be shown what structure this backup has. Click the **NEXT** button.

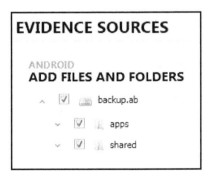

The structure of the backup.ad file in the window of the AXIOM Process program

3. Click the **GO TO PROCESSING DETAILS** button.

4. In the next window, you will be prompted to specify the additional criteria for processing the examined file, such as: add keywords, to calculate for the detected hash files or not, set criteria of detected images separation, and so on. When you set the parameters you want, click the **GO TO ARTIFACT DETAILS** button. In the next window, you will be prompted to select the categories of artifacts that you need to find in the backup.

5. Since physical dumps and backups of mobile devices are small enough, the search for them will not take much time, even if in this window the parameter that the program should search for all possible artifacts is set.

6. When the artifacts that have to be found during the process of analysis are specified, click on the **GO TO ANALYZE EVIDENCE** button and then on the **ANALYZE EVIDENCE** button. It will start the analysis process, the progress of which will be displayed in the **AXION Process** window, and the artifacts found during the process of analysis of the backup will be displayed in the **AXIOM Examine** window. The **AXIOM Examine** window will be opened automatically when the analysis of the backup is started. When the analysis is finished, the **AXIOM Process** window can be closed.

ALL EVIDENCE	**32,343**
REFINED RESULTS	**8,340**
EMAIL	**7,130**
WEB RELATED	**3,481**
MOBILE	**1,209**
Android Call Logs	639
Calendar Events	48
Installed Applications	22
Samsung Text Message Logs	500
MEDIA	**12,017**
Carved Video	26
Pictures	11.985
Videos	6
DOCUMENTS	**23**
OPERATING SYSTEM	**143**
Android Downloads	143

Information about the extracted data

It is convenient to view and do a primary analysis of the data in the **AXIOM Examine** window. Also, you can generate forensic reports both for all extracted data, and for a selected category via AXIOM Examine.

See also

- The website of the Magnet Forensics company: `https://www.magnetforensics. com/`

Android physical dumps parsing with Encase Forensic

As mentioned before, classical tools for computer forensics also increase their functionality in the examination of mobile devices. This is due to the fact that every year the number of mobile devices that come for examination to forensic laboratories increases. It means that experts need software for their analysis. Encase Forensic is following this trend. If we take a look at User Manual Encase Forensic, we can see that one third of this document is dedicated to the mobile devices' data extraction and analysis, their physical dumps, and backups. Encase Forensic can extract data from Android mobile devices and analyze their backups and physical dumps.

In this chapter, we will describe the analysis of an Android mobile device's backup via Encase Forensic.

Getting ready

Unfortunately, there is no public trial version of this program. It is possible to receive the license of the program for a certain period from resellers and partners of the company. In the versions 7 and 8 of this program, it became possible to activate the digital license that makes the installation of the program much easier. Install the program by double clicking on the icon of the installation file. Follow the installation instructions. Plug in the hardware key to your computer and activate the digital license using the appropriate instruction.

How to do it...

1. Double-click the icon of the program. Pay attention to the title of the program window when it starts. If the title of the program window says **Encase Forensic**, then the program runs in full-function mode. If the title of the window says **Encase Acquire**, it means that the program did not find the license.

2. To get started, you will need to create a new case. In the program toolbar, select **Case | New Case ....** In the opened **Options** window, fill in the **Name** field and click the **OK** button. Next, in the toolbar, select **Add Evidence | Acquire Smartphone ...**, as shown in the following screenshot:

The appearance of the drop-down Add Evidence menu

3. In the opened **Acquire Smartphone** window, select the type of **Evidence** as **Android Backup**, specify the path to the backup of the Android mobile device, the path and the file's name, where the file of the Encase program with extracted data will be saved. Click the **Finish** button.

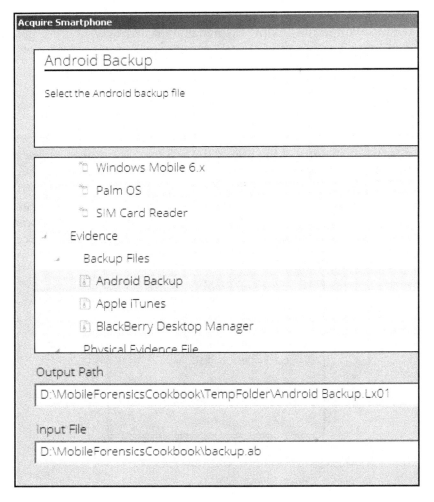

The appearance of the Acquire Smartphone window

4. When the analysis is finished, its results will be presented in a form familiar to any expert working with the Encase Forensic program.

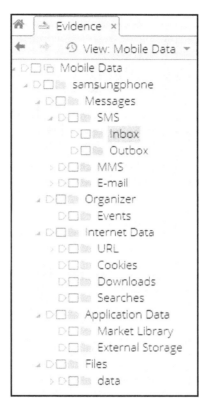

Results of the data extraction from the backup of an Android mobile device

See also

- Th website of the Encase Forensic program: `https://www.guidancesoftware.com/`

Thumbnails analysis with ThumbnailExpert

Any expert understands the importance of analyzing the thumbnail databases of graphics files and video files on the device. As well as on computers, similar bases can be found on Android mobile devices. The complexity of their examination is that its bases have different names and are saved on different paths (depending on the Android version). Even before the option of such bases analysis appeared in mobile forensics tools, in our forensic laboratory, ThumbnailExpert was used for detection and analysis of such databases.

ThumbnailExpert is designed to search for unusual thumbnail databases of graphics files created by various computer programs, but in addition to the extraction and analysis of thumbnail databases of the programs that are known to the tool, you can also search for new thumbnail databases. In order to search for such bases on an Android mobile device, you should copy the partition "user" filesystem from your mobile device to your computer or, for example, to a flash drive. This procedure must be done before the analysis.

Getting ready

Unfortunately, at the moment, this project does not have its own website. You can get a trial version or buy it by contacting the author. Download and unzip the archive. Double click on the program's file. Accept the license agreement by ticking the box '**I accept the agreement**' and click the '**OK**' button.

How to do it...

1. Double click the icon of the program. When the program is started, click on the **Open** option of the program's toolbar, and in the drop-down menu, tick the box next to **Search images in files of an unknown format** and **Skip standard images**:

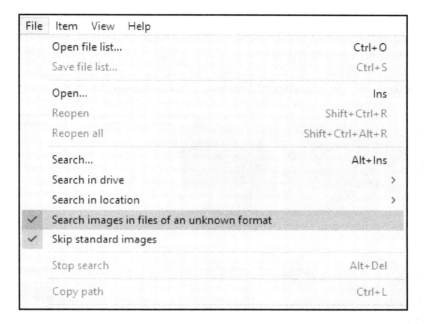

Setting search parameters

2. In the same menu, you need to specify the location, meaning the place where the program will search for the files of thumbnail databases. Use **Search in drive** or **Search in location** options for this. When the place where the files will be searched for is specified, the search will start. The progress of the search will be displayed in the progress bar, which is located in the lower part of the window.

3. When the analysis is finished, in the left part of the main window of the program, the files that contain the graphics files will be displayed. The number of graphics thumbnails contained in the file is mentioned in parentheses:

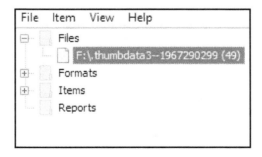

Results of the analysis

4. In the main window of the program, the detected thumbnails will be displayed. They can be viewed. You can generate the report for all detected thumbnails or only for thumbnails tagged by an expert. Also, if the thumbnails have headers, and similar headers of the graphics file in JPG format, the program can extract metadata, which will also be presented in the report, from the headers.

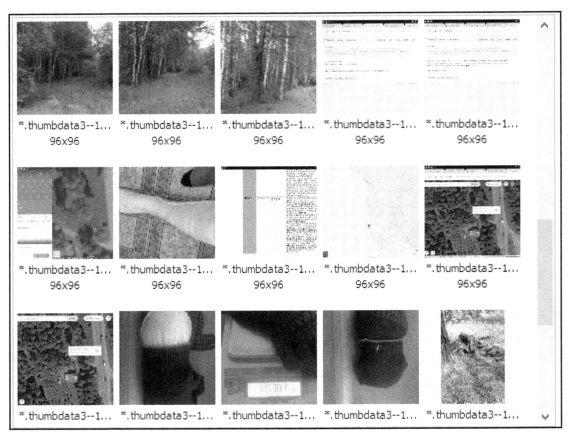

Detected thumbnails

There's more...

- The article *Do not miss new thumbnail databases in Android OS* can be found at:
  `https://www.digitalforensics.com/blog/do-not-miss-new-thumbnail-databases-in-android-os/`

See also

- The trial version of the ThumbnailExpert program: `http://web.archive.org/web/20110717053520/http://www.thumbnailexpert.com/binary/ThumbnailExpertEn.zip`
- The website if the program's author: `http://www.ithmbconverter.com/`

9
iOS Forensics

In this chapter, we'll cover the following recipes:

- iOS backup parsing with iPhone Backup Extractor
- iOS backup parsing with UFED Physical Analyzer
- iOS backup parsing with BlackLight
- iOS physical dump and backup parsing with Oxygen Forensic
- iOS backup parsing with Belkasoft Evidence Center
- iOS backup parsing with AXIOM
- iOS backup parsing with Encase Forensic
- iOS backup parsing with Elcomsoft Phone Viewer
- Thumbnail analysis with iThmb Converter

Introduction

The main sources of data extracted from Apple mobile devices are:

- Physical dumps
- Filesystems
- Backups

Physical dumps and filesystems are the minimum part of all objects that come for analysis to forensic laboratories. This is due to the security mechanisms used in Apple mobile devices. The vast majority of objects are backups. iTunes is an Apple company tool that is used for backup creation on Apple mobile devices. Forensic tools, overtly or covertly from the expert, also basically extract data from Apple's mobile devices indirectly: first, they create an iTunes backup, and then they extract data from it.

Backups can be found on the following paths:

- **mac OS X:** `C:\Users\<User Name>\Library\Application Support \ MobileSync\Backup\`
- **Windows XP:** `C:\Documents and Setting\<User Name>\ Application Data\Apple Computer\MobileSync\Backup\`
- **Windows Vista, 7, 8, and 10:** `C:\Users\<User Name>\AppData\ Roaming\Apple Computer\MobileSync\Backup\`

iTunes backups can have different formats depending on the version of the iOS operating system installed in the examined device.

Name ▲	Date modified	Type	Size
68	9/26/2017 1:48 PM	File folder	
69	9/26/2017 1:48 PM	File folder	
70	9/26/2017 1:48 PM	File folder	
71	9/26/2017 1:48 PM	File folder	
72	9/26/2017 1:48 PM	File folder	
73	9/26/2017 1:48 PM	File folder	
74	9/26/2017 1:48 PM	File folder	
Info.plist	9/13/2017 7:20 PM	PLIST File	426 KB
Manifest	9/13/2017 7:19 PM	Data Base File	8,061 KB
Manifest.plist	9/13/2017 7:19 PM	PLIST File	28 KB
Status.plist	9/13/2017 7:19 PM	PLIST File	1 KB

Appearance of iTunes backup of device with operating system iOS 10 version or higher

Sometimes you can face a situation where the examined iTunes backup is encrypted. It happens when the owner of the device used an encryption option when they created backups.

Name ▲	Date modified	Type	Size
ff7214a6200f93dc5eb839aa68ed56011cb8e…	8/16/2017 3:45 PM	File	43 KB
ff8525fcd5780ab29d64e00f6bef5a37b55ba…	8/16/2017 3:45 PM	File	7 KB
ffb8647db025c77e7191c649d4192085d2f4f…	8/16/2017 3:47 PM	File	1 KB
ffbb71cd47409a6f86b64bb19d0ed2c6240ba…	8/16/2017 3:47 PM	File	1 KB
ffcc3a0719ea5b53b720a2b0ccdacaea75336…	8/16/2017 3:46 PM	File	1,039 KB
ffec0f015427a9464526de85c6d16cf00b258…	8/16/2017 3:46 PM	File	1 KB
ffff64402524baf7d1e3bc49780379e69fe69ed0	8/16/2017 3:47 PM	File	13 KB
Info.plist	8/16/2017 3:48 PM	PLIST File	1,257 KB
Manifest.mbdb	8/16/2017 3:48 PM	MBDB File	1,867 KB
Manifest.plist	8/16/2017 3:48 PM	PLIST File	26 KB
Status.plist	8/16/2017 3:48 PM	PLIST File	1 KB

Appearance of iTunes backup of device with operating system iOS lower than version 10

If you cannot find out the password from the owner of the device, you can use the Elcomsoft Phone Breaker or Passware Kit Forensic programs to restore it. If you have access to the Mac, Macbook, or Mac Air of the mobile device owner, the backup password can be extracted from the keychain of these computers and laptops.

iOS backup parsing with iPhone Backup Extractor

iPhone Backup Extractor is a shareware tool. You can extract data from iTunes backups, including encrypted ones, via this tool.

Getting ready

Download the tool from the developer's website. Double-click on the icon of the downloaded file. Follow the instructions to install the program:

1. Double-click on the icon of installed iPhone Backup Extractor program. When the program has started, you need to create your account. Click **ACTIVATE**; the button is located in the right upper corner of the program's window:

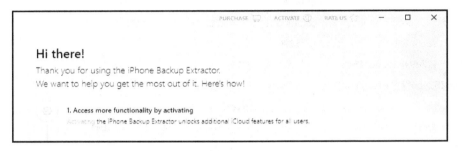

The appearance of a fragment of the iPhone Backup Extractor window

2. In the opened additional window, click **Create a free account**. In the next window, fill in these fields: **Your email address**, **Password**, and **Repeat password**. Click the **CREATE ACCOUNT** button:

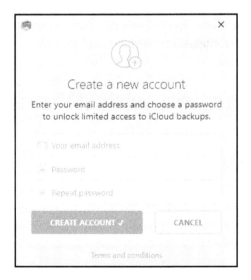

Appearance of the new account creation window

3. You will receive an email to the email address specified during registration, in order to confirm the email address. Click the **Verify address** button to create the account:

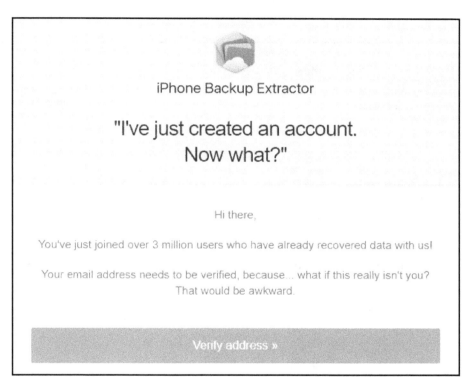

iPhone Backup Extractor

"I've just created an account.
Now what?"

Hi there,

You've just joined over 3 million users who have already recovered data with us!

Your email address needs to be verified, because... what if this really isn't you? That would be awkward.

Verify address »

Fragment of an email received from Reincubate Ltd

Congratulations. Your account has been created.

4. Click **ACTIVATE** one more time on the window of the iPhone Backup Extractor program. In the opened additional window, enter email and password. Click the arrow icon. The **UNREGISTERED** inscription at the top part of the program's window should change to the email address specified during the account registration process.

How to do it...

1. In order to upload an iTunes backup to the program, click on the + icon that is located on the desktop of the program:

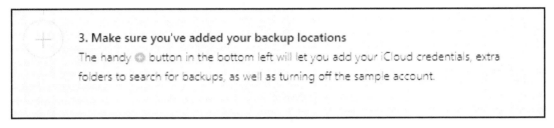

3. Make sure you've added your backup locations

The handy ⚙ button in the bottom left will let you add your iCloud credentials, extra folders to search for backups, as well as turning off the sample account.

+ icon

2. In the opened **Preferences** window, you will be shown the path where iTunes backups are stored, if they were created by the iTunes program with default settings.
3. If you click the + icon that is located in the lower left corner of the program, you can specify the path to iTunes backups located elsewhere on your computer's hard drive:

Preferences ✕

GENERAL ⚙   ICLOUD

We always look for backups in your default folder.
If you store backups in other folders you can add them below:

C:\Users\User\AppData\Roaming\Apple Computer\MobileSync\Backup

C:\Users\User\Documents\efa59d0d81ec8be088e5b587d53fc6fa8189c0fd

Fragment of the Preferences window

4. When you specify the path to the iTunes backup, iPhone Backup Extractor will start the backup analysis. The analysis results will be displayed in the main window of the program. Close the window by clicking the **x** icon that is located in the top right part of the **Preferences** window:

A window of iPhone Backup Extractor with the iTunes backup analysis results

You can view the data contained in the examined iTunes backup by clicking on the icons of categories.

iPhone Backup Extractor can extract iTunes backups from iCloud. If an iTunes backup is encrypted, you will be prompted to enter the password. The program will decrypt the backup using the provided password.

See also

- Website of the iPhone Backup Extractor program: https://www. iphonebackupextractor.com

iOS backup parsing with UFED Physical Analyzer

UFED Physical Analyzer is a tool that is provided together with Cellebrite products such as UFED 4PC, UFED Touch, UFED Touch 2, UFED UME-36, and so on. Using this tool, you can analyze the following extracted data: physical dumps, backups, and filesystems of mobile devices, and also you can extract data from Apple mobile devices and from GPS/mass storage devices. UFED Physical Analyzer includes SQLite Wizard, which we described in `Chapter 7`, *Understanding Plist Forensics*.

Getting ready

You can request a trial license of UFED Physical Analyzer from Cellebrite distributors. In response to the request, you will receive an email with links to the distribution kits. Download UFED Physical Analyzer. Double-click the icon for the setup file of the program. Follow the instructions to install UFED Physical Analyzer. When the installation is finished, click the icon for UFED Physical Analyzer.

When the program has started, it will show a window that indicates that the program is not activated.

Click **Software**. In the new window, you will find the computer's ID, which you need to send to the distributor.

In response to your email with the computer's ID, you will receive a new email, which will contain links to the license files and activation instructions.

Follow the instruction to activate UFED Physical Analyzer.

How to do it...

1. Double-click the icon for UFED Physical Analyzer. In the toolbar, click **File |
   Open (Advanced)**. In the **Open (Advanced)** window, click the **Select
   Device** button:

Selection of the type of extraction

2. Select **Apple iOS iTunes (Backup)**. Click the **Next** button and then **Next** again. In the next window, click the **Folder** button, and specify the path to the iTunes backup. Click the **Open** button. Click **Finish**. The process of analysis will start. When the analysis process is finished, the results of it will be displayed in the program's window:

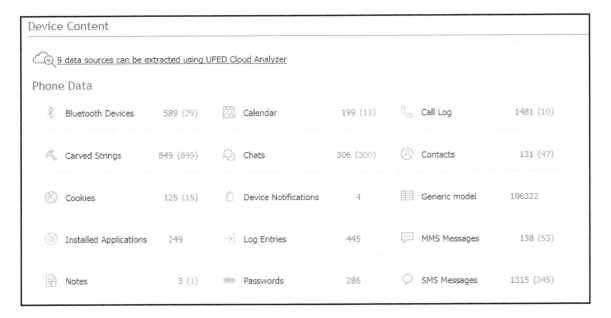

Device Content

9 data sources can be extracted using UFED Cloud Analyzer

Phone Data

Bluetooth Devices	589 (29)	Calendar	199 (11)	Call Log	1481 (10)
Carved Strings	849 (849)	Chats	306 (300)	Contacts	131 (47)
Cookies	125 (15)	Device Notifications	4	Generic model	196322
Installed Applications	249	Log Entries	445	MMS Messages	138 (53)
Notes	3 (1)	Passwords	286	SMS Messages	1315 (345)

Results of analysis of data extracted from iTunes backup

UFED Cloud Analyzer can extract iTunes backups from iCloud. If an iTunes backup is encrypted, you will be prompted to enter the password. The program will decrypt the backup using the provided password.

iOS backup parsing with BlackLight

BlackLight is a tool from BlackBag Technologies, Inc. BlackLight can be used for the analysis of hard drives of computers or laptops running Windows or macOS. Using BlackLight, you can acquire and analyze Android and Apple mobile devices.

Getting ready

Request the demo version of the program. In response to the request, you will receive a link to download the trial version of the program and the activation code. Download the installation file. Double-click on it. Follow the instruction to install the program. Double-click the icon for BlackLight. In the opened **Dongle Required** window, click the **Enter Demo Key...** button. Fill in the **Name** and ;**License** fields and click the **OK** button. Restart the program.

How to do it...

1. In the **BlackLight Case Manager** window, click the **New...** button and enter the name of the new case. Click the **Save** button. Fill in the fields of the **Examiner Information** and **Case Information** sections. In the program toolbar, select **File**. In the drop-down menu, select **Add Evidence ....**

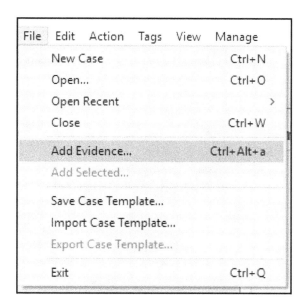

Fragment of the main BlackLight window

2. Click the **Add** icon that is located next to the **Files/Folders/Disk Images** inscription.

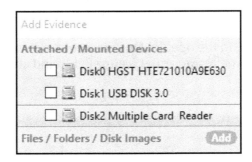

Fragment of the Add Evidence window.

3. In the opened additional window, click the **Add Folder....** Select the folder where the iTunes backup is stored and click the **Open** button. The information about the selected backup will be displayed in the **Add Evidence** window:

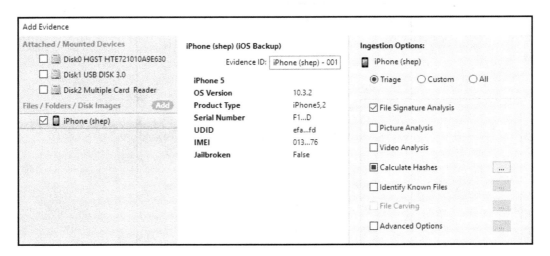

Fragment of the Add Evidence window

4. Select the ingestion options by ticking the appropriate boxes in the **Add Evidence** window. Click the **Start** button.
5. The analysis of the selected iTunes backup will start. The analysis progress will be displayed in the lower part of the main BlackLight window.

6. When the analysis process is finished, you will be able to view the results by clicking on the icons of the BlackLight toolbar or by clicking on the categories in the **Artefacts** section of the main BlackLight window:

Icons on the BlackLight toolbar

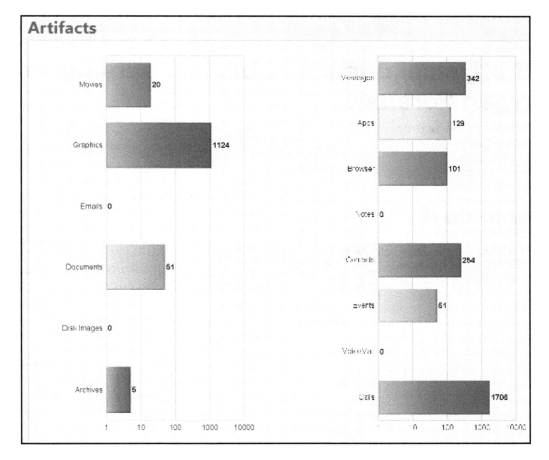

Appearance of the Artefacts section

If an iTunes backup is encrypted, you will be prompted to enter the password. The program will decrypt the backup using the provided password.

See also

- Website of the BlackLight company: `https://www.blackbagtech.com/software-products.html`

iOS physical dump and backup parsing with Oxygen Forensic

The Oxygen Forensic program has already been described in Chapter 1, *SIM Cards Acquisition and Analysis*. In this recipe, we will show how to analyze an iTunes backup via Oxygen Forensic.

How to do it...

1. In order to import data from an iTunes backup, click the arrow to the right of the **Import file** button on the Oxygen Forensic toolbar. In the drop-down menu, go to **Import Apple backup/image** and then **Import iTunes backup ....**

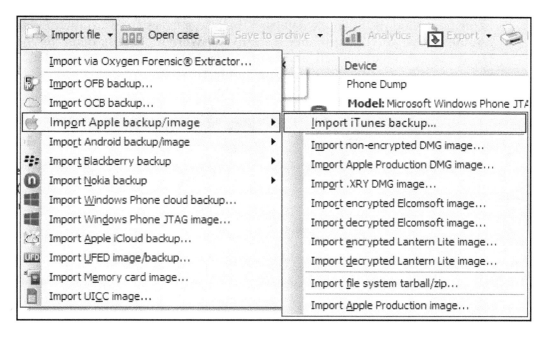

Selection of the data import type

2. In the opened window, specify the path to the backup copy. Select the
   `Manifest.plist` file and click the **Open** file.

3. In the new window, fill in the details of the case, such as **Case number, Evidence number, Place, Incident number, Backup password** (optional), **Inspector, Device owner, Owner email**, and so on. If you need to recover deleted data, tick **Search and recover deleted data from applications**. The process of data restoration will take additional time. Click the **Next** button:

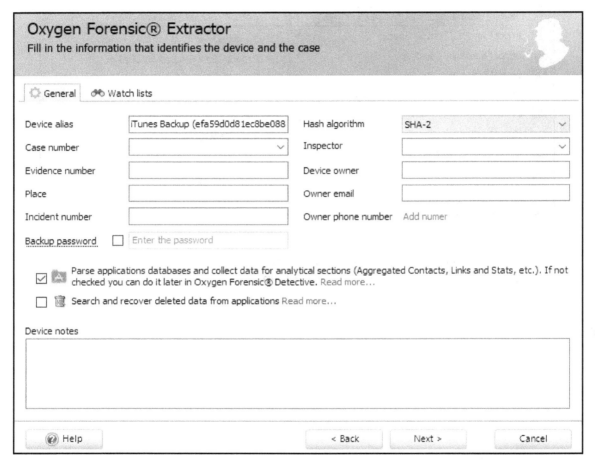

Window of Oxygen Forensic Extractor with information about the case and extraction's option

4. The program will prompt you to double-check the entered data by displaying it in the window. If all the data is correct, click the **Extract** button. The import process will start:

Oxygen Forensic® Extractor

Importing C:\Users\User\Documents\efa59d0d81ec8be088e5b587d53fc6fa8189c0fd\Manifest.plist

Data extraction from iTunes backup

Extracting data from "C:\Users\User\Documents\efa59d0d81ec8be088e5b587d53fc6fa8189c0fd"

/private/var/mobile/Media/DCIM/101APPLE/IMG_1279.MOV

Process of data import

5. When the data import is finished, the final window of Oxygen Forensic Extractor with summary information about the import will be displayed:

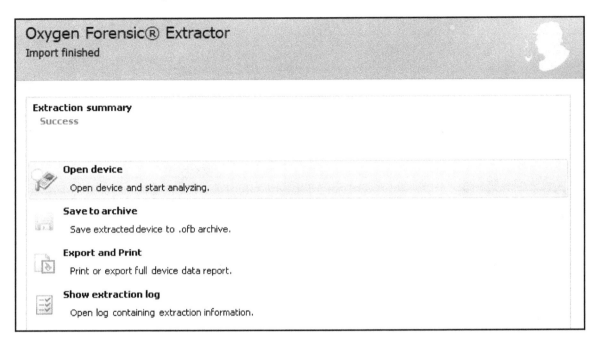

Window with summary information

6. Click **Finish** to finish the data extraction. You will be able to view the information about the extracted data that was found during the analysis process in the main window of the Oxygen Forensic program:

The analysis results

Oxygen Forensic can extract iTunes backups from iCloud. Oxygen Forensic can extract data from iTunes backups that are protected by passwords. The tool of the Passware company is used for recovery of iTunes backup passwords. The tool is included in the installation kit of Oxygen Forensic.

iOS backup parsing with Belkasoft Evidence Center

The Belkasoft Evidence Center program has already been described in `Chapter 6`, *SQLite Forensics*. In this recipe, we will describe how to analyze an iTunes backup via Belkasoft Evidence Center.

How to do it...

1. Start the Belkasoft Evidence Center program. Click the **New Case** button. Specify the information about the new case, such as the name of the case, the path, where the data of the case will be located, the name of the investigator, a description of the case, and the time zone. Click on the **Create and open** button:

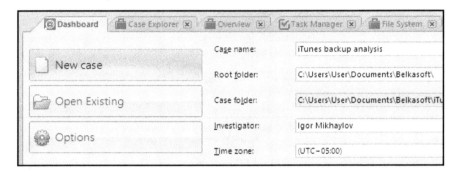

The window of a new case setting

2. In the next window, specify the path to the iTunes backup that was extracted earlier. Select the `Manifest.plist` file. Click the **Open** button and then the **Next** button:

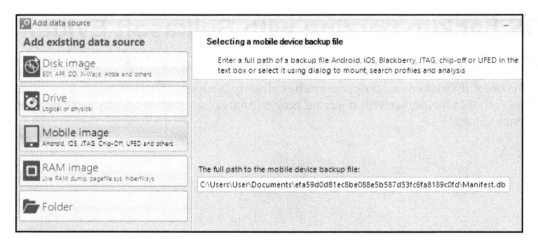

Selection window of data source

3. Specify the types of data (chats, email messages images, videos, calls, SMS messages, and so on) that you need to extract. Click the **Finish** button. The more types of data specified for extraction, the longer the analysis process will take. As a rule, the analysis time is not critical for the analysis of backups of mobile devices. The analysis of the device used as an example took 12 minutes:

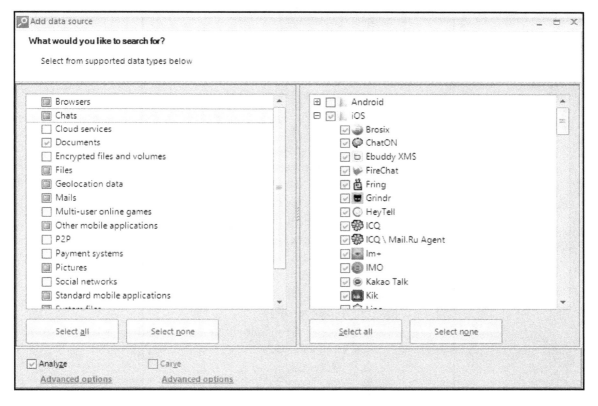

Selection window of the types of data to be found

4. The detected types of data will be displayed when the analysis process is finished:

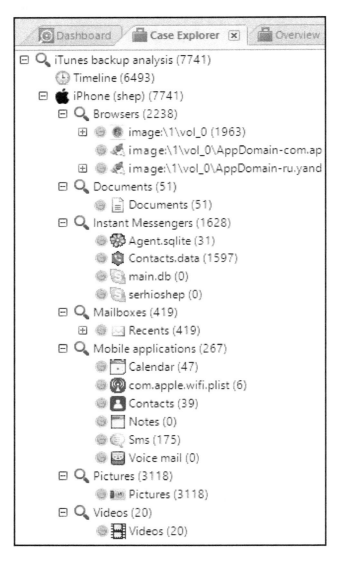

Types of data extracted from the examined backup of an Apple mobile device

Despite the fact that the created backup copy contains only the data that is stored on the device in an explicit form, during the analysis process the following types of data are recovered: deleted records from the phonebook, calls, chats, deleted SMS messages, and notes. Analyzing thumbnails of graphics and video files, it is possible to understand what pictures and video was on the examined device. Extracted and recovered data can be viewed and analyzed in the Belkasoft Evidence Center program. Also, you can create reports that can be provided to the court as evidence.

iOS backup parsing with AXIOM

The AXIOM program has already been described in `Chapter 8`, *Analyzing Physical Dumps and Backups of Android Devices*. In this recipe, we will describe how to analyze an iTunes backup via AXIOM.

How to do it...

1. Double-click the AXIOM Process icon. In the program's window, click the **CREATE NEW CASE** button. In the next window, fill in the case information fields, such as **Case number**, **Folder name**, **File path**, and **Scanned by**, then click the **GO TO EVIDENCE SOURCES** button. In the next window, in the **SELECT EVIDENCE SOURCE** section, click the MOBILE icon. In the next window, click the IOS icon:

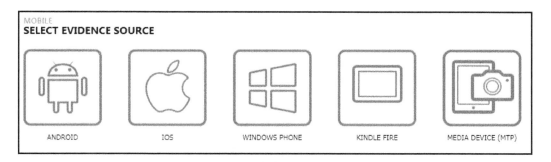

SELECT EVIDENCE SOURCE (MOBILE) section

2. In the next window, click the LOAD EVIDENCE icon. In the next window, click on the FILES & FOLDERS icon. In the opened additional **EVIDENCE SOURCES** window, click the **WINDOWS FOLDER BROWSER** button. Specify the path to the iTunes backup to be examined and click the **Select Folder** button.

3. Click the **GO TO PROCESSING DETAILS** button. In the next window, you will be prompted to set additional criteria for processing the examined file, such as keywords, whether to calculate hash for the detected files or not, the criteria for detected image separation, and so on. When you have set all the parameters you need, click **GO TO ARTIFACT DETAILS**. In the next window, you will be prompted to select the categories of artifacts that are to be found in the examined backup. Click the **CUSTOMIZE ARTIFACTS** button and select the types of artifacts you need to find in the iTunes backup:

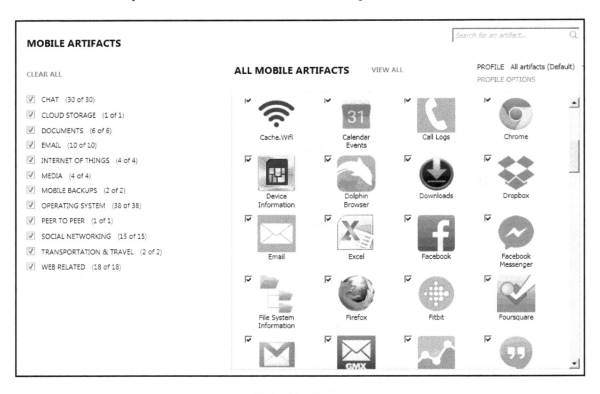

Selection of the artifact types

4. Once the artifacts are selected, click the **GO TO ANALYZE EVIDENCE** button and then the **ANALYZE EVIDENCE** button. The analysis process will start, the progress of which will be displayed in the AXIOM Process window. The artifacts found during the process of backup analysis will be displayed in the AXIOM Examine window. Since iTunes backups are small, their examination process does not take a lot of time.

AXIOM Examine is automatically opened when the analysis process is started. When the analysis process is finished, the window of AXIOM Process can be closed. The results of the analysis can be viewed in the main window of AXIOM Examine:

ALL EVIDENCE	**11,601**
REFINED RESULTS	**622**
CHAT	**291**
iOS iMessage/SMS/MMS	290
Skype Accounts	1
WEB RELATED	**2,578**
MOBILE	**3,475**
Calendar Events	47
iOS Call Logs	3,366
iOS Contacts	39
iOS Notes - Voice	14
iOS User Shortcut Dictionary	2
iOS Wi-Fi Profiles	6
Owner Information	1
MEDIA	**4,587**
DOCUMENTS	**47**
OPERATING SYSTEM	**1**

The results of the iTunes backup analysis

It is convenient to view and make primary analysis of the extracted data. Also, using AXIOM Examine you can generate forensic reports both for all extracted data and for a certain selected category.

> If an iTunes backup is encrypted, you will be prompted to enter the password. The program will decrypt the backup using the provided password.

iOS backup parsing with Encase Forensic

The Encase Forensic program has already been described in `Chapter 8`, *Analyzing Physical Dumps and Backups of Android Devices*. In this recipe, we will describe how to analyze an iTunes backup via Encase Forensic.

How to do it...

1. Double-click the icon of the program. Pay attention to the title of the program window when it starts. If the title of the program window says **Encase Forensic**, then the program runs in full-function mode. If the title of the window says **Encase Acquire**, it means that the program did not find the license.
2. To get started, you will need to create a new case. In the program's toolbar, select **Case | New Case ....** In the opened **Options** window, fill in the **Name** field and click the **OK** button. Then, in the toolbar, select **Add Evidence | Acquire Mobile | Acquire From File....**.

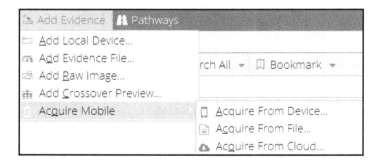

Appearance of the Add Evidence drop-down menu

3. In the opened **Output File Settings**, fill in the following fields: **Notes, Evidence Number**, and **Examiner Name**. Specify the path to the folder, where the files of Encase program with extracted data will be saved, and click the **OK** button.

4. In the **Import Wizard** window, tick **iPhone Backup**. Click the **Next** button:

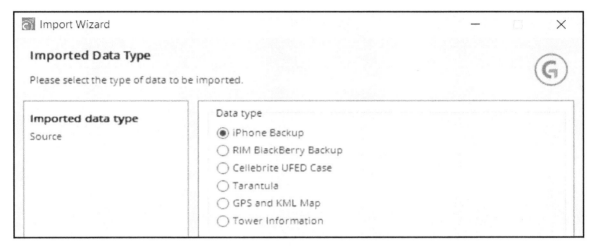

Fragment of the Import Wizard window

5. Click the **Browse...** button and specify the path to the folder where the iTunes backup is stored. Select the `Manifest.plist` file and click the **Open** button, and then **Finish**:

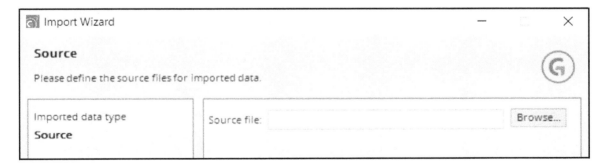

Fragment of the Import Wizard window

6. The process of data extraction from the examined backup will start. The progress of it will be displayed in the **Import Wizard** window:

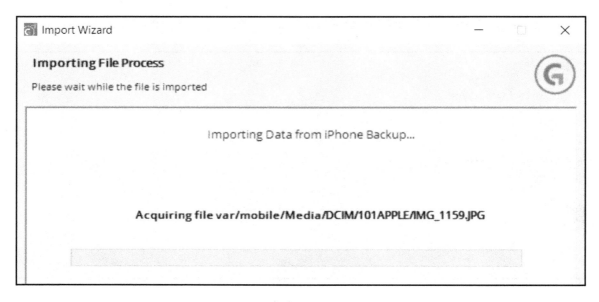

The progress of the data extraction process from the iTunes backup

7. When the extraction process is finished, a message about the successful import from the backup to Encase Forensic will be displayed in the **Import Wizard** window. Click the **Finish** button:

A message about the successful import of the iTunes backup

8. The imported data will be added to the opened case in this program. The progress of the data import to the case will be displayed in the right lower corner of the main window of Encase Forensic.

9. When the analysis is finished, its results will be presented in a form familiar to any expert working with the Encase Forensic program:

- Mobile Data
  - iTunes
    - iPhone Backup
      - Parsed Data
        - Voice Memo
        - Cookies
        - Calendar
        - Contacts
        - Call History
        - Notes
        - Address Book Images
        - Safari Bookmarks
        - Safari History
        - Messages
      - Parsed Recovered Data
      - var
      - AppDomainPlugin-ru.beeline.mobile.wid
      - SysSharedContainerDomain-systemgrou
      - AppDomainPlugin-ru.yandex.mobile.key
      - AppDomainPlugin-ru.difree.Ruble.Ruble\
      - AppDomainPlugin-com.vk.vkclient.share
      - AppDomainPlugin-ru.odnoklassniki.ipho
      - SysSharedContainerDomain-systemgrou
      - AppDomainPlugin-com.6wunderkinder.w
      - SysSharedContainerDomain-systemgrou
      - AppDomainPlugin-com.evernote.iPhone.
      - AppDomainPlugin-com.viber.SiriExtensic

Results of the data extraction from the iTunes backup

iOS backup parsing with Elcomsoft Phone Viewer

Elcomsoft Phone Viewer is a tool from Elcomsof Co.Ltd. Using this tool, you can extract data from iCloud and iTunes, and BlackBerry backups. This program has a low price. In this recipe, we will describe how to analyze an iTunes backup via Elcomsoft Phone Viewer.

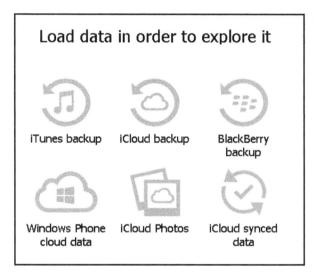

Data types available for import to Elcomsoft Phone Viewer

Getting ready

Download the tool from the link sent to you and double-click on the installation file icon. Follow the instructions to install the program. During the installation process, you will be prompted to enter the registration code. Enter the registration code sent to you and click the **Next** button. Finish the installation of the program.

How to do it...

1. Double-click the icon of the Elcomsoft Phone Viewer. In the main window of the program, click on the icon with the iTunes backup inscription.

2. In the opened **Select iOS backup for view** window, specify the path to the folder where the iTunes backup is stored. Select the `Manifest.plist` file and click the **Open** button.

3. The program will display an additional window with a clarification request for whether you want to find all media files, including those contained in third-party applications or not. If you want it, click **Yes**, if do not, click **No**:

Window with the clarification request

4. The process of the iTunes backup analysis will start, the progress of which will be displayed in the main window of the program:

Progress of the data extraction process

5. When the extraction process is finished, the results will be displayed in the main window of the program. You can view the data that is contained in the examined backup by clicking the icons of categories:

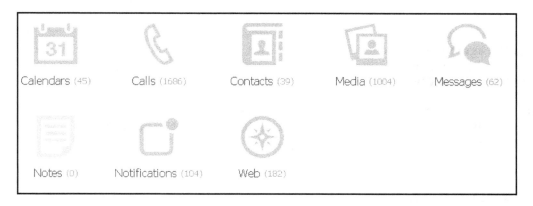

Calendars (45)   Calls (1686)   Contacts (39)   Media (1004)   Messages (62)

Notes (0)   Notifications (104)   Web (182)

Results of the iTunes backup analysis

See also

* The website of Elcomsoft Phone Viewer: https://www.elcomsoft.com/epv.html

Thumbnail analysis with iThmb Converter

If an Apple mobile device user synchronized it using iTunes, then in this device you can find files with the ITHMB extension. These files serve to create thumbnail galleries that speed up the process of image viewing. The graphics file thumbnails contained in the ITHMB files also contain EXIF sections, which makes their identification much easier. It can also help experts to find other devices that contain these graphic files.

iThmb Converter allows extracting thumbnails of graphics files and their EXIF sections from ITHMB files.

Getting ready

Two versions of the program are available for downloading: the installation file and the portable version. Go to the program's website and download it. Double-click on the downloaded file. Follow the instructions to install the program. When the installation is finished, the license agreement will be displayed. Read it. If you agree to the terms, tick **I accept the agreement** and click **OK**. On first start, you will be shown an information window, which will inform you that the program is not licensed and is running in demo mode. Click the **OK** button.

If you have the license code, go to the **Help | Registration** option in the toolbar of the program. Enter the code in the additional **Please enter the registration key** window. Click **OK**. Restart the program.

How to do it...

1. The main window of the program has three sections:
2. Section 1 (located on the left) has a tree structure, like Windows Explorer. Using this section, you can navigate through local drives and folders:

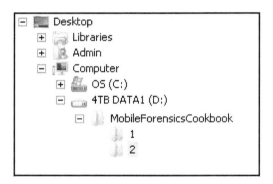

The appearance of section 1

3. Section 2 (located in the middle) displays the names of all files with the ITHMB extension that are located in the selected folder:

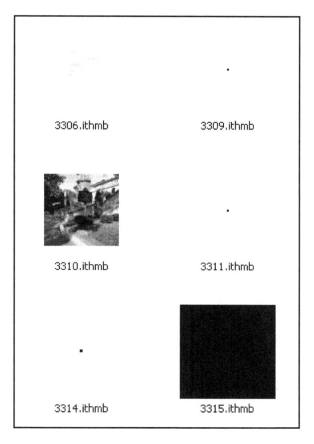

The appearance of section 2

4. Section 3 (located on the right) displays the thumbnails of the files, which is contained in the selected ITHMB file:

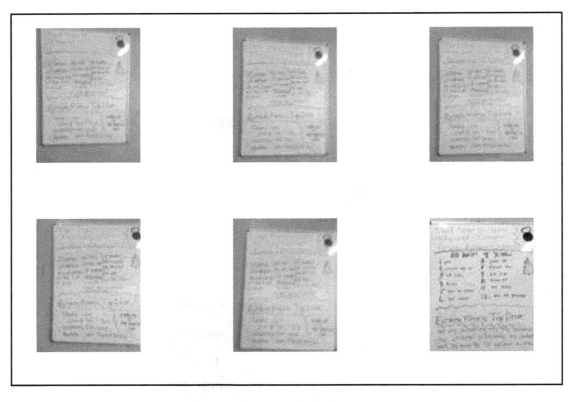

The appearance of section 3

5. Select the folder where the ITHMB files are contained in section 1. Select the ITHMB file you need in section 2. View the thumbnails contained in the file in section 3.

See also

- The website of the iThmb Converter program: http://www.ithmbconverter.com/

10
Windows Phone and BlackBerry Forensics

In this chapter, we'll cover the following recipes:

- BlackBerry backup parsing with Elcomsoft Blackberry Backup Explorer Pro
- BlackBerry backup parsing with Oxygen Forensic
- Windows Phone physical dump and backup parsing with Oxygen Forensic
- Windows Phone physical dump parsing with UFED Physical Analyzer

Introduction

Backup copy creation is the main method of data extraction from mobile devices running BlackBerry OS. On computers running Windows OS, backups of mobile devices running BlackBerry OS are created via BlackBerry Desktop Software or BlackBerry Link. Backup copies have a `.bbb` extension (in MacOS, backup copies have a `.ipd` extension).

Backup copies are saved on the following paths:

- Windows XP: `C:\Documents and Settings\<UserName>\My Documents\`
- Windows Vista, Windows 7, Windows 8, Windows 10: `C:\Users\<UserName>\Documents \`

The backup files have the following names:

- A backup created manually using the **Backup and Restore** option of the **BlackBerry Desktop Software»** program: **Backup- (yyyy-mm-dd) .bbb"** *
- A backup created via the application loading wizard of the **BlackBerry Desktop Software LoaderBackup-(yyyy-mm-dd) .bbb»** *
- A backup created automatically: **AutoBackup- (yyyy-mm-dd) .bbb***

   * yyyy-mm-dd is year-month-day.

Backups of BlackBerry OS 10 are encrypted. In order to extract data from them, you will need the BlackBerry ID and password of the mobile device owner.

To create a full copy of a mobile device running the Windows Phone operating system, it is recommended to use the following methods:

- Create a copy of the mobile device memory using a special device management program in DFU mode. DFU (Device Firmware Upgrade) mode allows all devices to be restored from any state. This method is applicable for mobile devices released before 2014.
- Data extraction from the integrated memory chip via the debugging interface JTAG (Joint Test Action Group).
- Data extraction from the integrated memory chip using the In-System Programming (ISP) method.
- Data extraction from the memory chip (Chip-off).

It should be mentioned that:

- For Windows Phone devices, starting with the x30 series, data extraction via the debugging interface (JTAG) is not available, as the test points have been removed from their system boards. On the other hand, the In-System Programming method became popular, which allows us to solder conductors directly to the memory chip on the system board of the mobile device and extract data much faster than the data extraction speed via the debug interface (JTAG).

- The method of data extraction from integrated memory chips (Chip-off) is a method that is used only when other methods did not provide the desired result. It is difficult to get the result as encryption of the user partition or lock code installed on the memory chip is used in mobile devices running the Windows Phone operating system. It is impossible to get access to the data that is stored in the integrated memory chip if you do not know the lock code installed on the memory chip.

BlackBerry backup parsing with Elcomsoft Blackberry Backup Explorer Pro

Elcomsoft Blackberry Backup Explorer Pro is a tool that is used for data extraction from Blackberry mobile devices running Blackberry OS. This tool does not support data extraction from encrypted backups that were created by devices running Blackberry OS 10. This program has a low price and anyone can purchase it.

Getting ready

Download the tool from the link sent to you and double-click on the installer icon. Follow the instructions to install the program. During the installation, you will be prompted to enter the license code. Enter the license code sent to you and click the **Next** button:

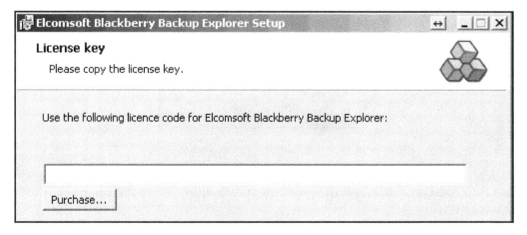

License code entry field

How to do it...

Double-click on the icon of the Elcomsoft Blackberry Backup Explorer Pro program. In the toolbar menu, click **File** and then in the opened menu click **Open IPB or BBB**, or you can also click **Open IPB or BBB**, which is located in the lower left corner of the program:

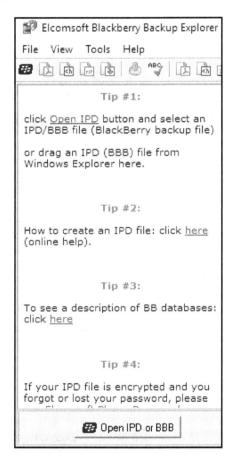

Fragment of the main window of Elcomsoft Blackberry Backup Explorer Pro

In the opened window, select the BlackBerry backup file (that has IPB or BBB extension) and click the **Open** button. When the file contents are uploaded to the program, it will be available for viewing:

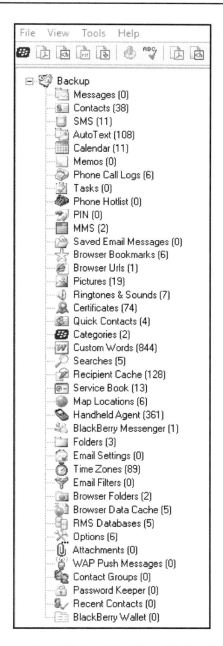

Categories of data extracted from the BlackBerry backup in Elcomsoft Blackberry Backup Explorer Pro

You can generate a report for a selected category of extracted data, in one of the available formats:

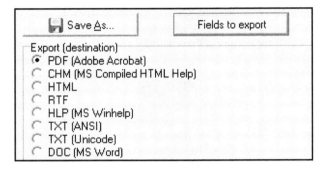

The bar of the main window of Elcomsoft Blackberry Backup Explorer Pro, in which you can specify the file extension in which the report will be generated

This report has custom fields that can be set by clicking the **Fields to export** button:

Window for field selection that will be presented in the report

 You can use Elcomsoft Phone Password Breaker (https://www.elcomsoft.com/eppb.html) for decryption of encrypted Blackberry backups (including backups for BlackBerry OS 10).

See also

- Website of the Elcomsoft Blackberry Backup Explorer Pro program: `https://www.elcomsoft.com/ebbe.html`

BlackBerry backup parsing with Oxygen Forensic

The Oxygen Forensic program has been described in `Chapter 1`, *SIM Cards Acquisition and Analysis*. In this recipe, we will describe the data extraction from a BlackBerry backup via Oxygen Forensic.

How to do it...

1. In order to import data from a backup, click the arrow that is located to the right of the **Import file** button on the Oxygen Forensic toolbar. In the drop-down menu, go to **Import Blackberry backup** and then **Import IPD backup ...**. If you have a different type of backup, select another option from this menu:

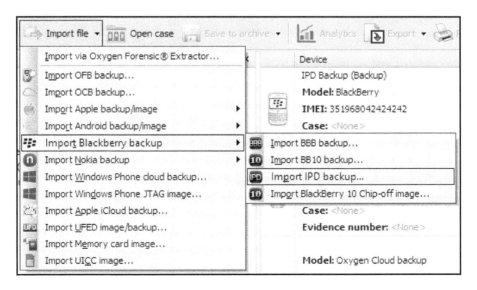

Selection of the type of data import

---

2. In the opened window, specify the path to the backup. Select the backup and click the **Open** button.

3. In the new window, fill in the details of the case, such as **Device alias, Case number, Evidence number, Place, Incident number, Inspector, Device owner,** and **Owner email.** Click the **Next** button:

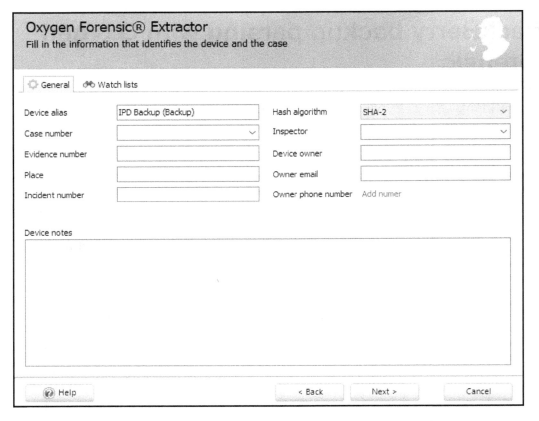

Window of the Oxygen Forensic Extractor program with information about the case and extraction options

4. The program will prompt you to double-check the entered data by displaying it in the window. If all the data is correct, click the **Extract** button. The import process will start.

5. When the data import is finished, the final window of Oxygen Forensic Extractor with summary information about the import will be displayed. Click the **Finish** button to finish the extraction.

6. The extracted data will be available for viewing and analysis:

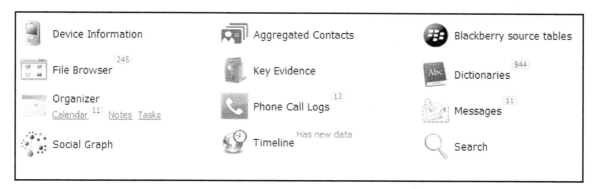

Information about the extracted data in the main window of the program

 If the BlackBerry backup that you upload to the Oxygen Forensic is encrypted, an additional window of the Oxygen Forensic Extractor program will be displayed, where you need to enter the BlackBerry ID and password of the examined device's owner.

Windows Phone physical dump and backup parsing with Oxygen Forensic

The Oxygen Forensic program has already been described in `Chapter 1`, *SIM Cards Acquisition and Analysis*. In this recipe, we will describe data extraction from the physical dump of Windows Phone via Oxygen Forensic.

How to do it...

1. Oxygen Forensic has functionality that allows you to recover the screen lock password from a physical dump of a Windows Phone device. A physical dump can be obtained by the JTAG and chip-off methods.

2. In order to import data from a Windows Phone physical dump, click the arrow that is located to the right of the **Import File** button on the Oxygen Forensic toolbar. In the drop-down menu, go to **Import Windows Phone JTAG image ....**

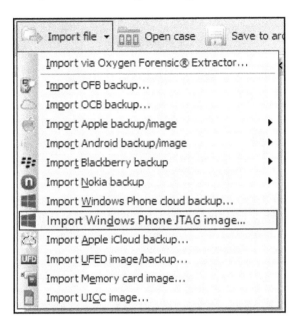

Selection of the type of data import

3. In the opened window, specify the path to the physical dump. Click the **Open** button.
4. In the new window, fill in the details of the case, such as **Device alias**, **Case number**, **Evidence number**, **Place**, **Incident number**, **Inspector**, **Device owner**, and **Owner email**. Click the **Next** button. If necessary, select the data that you want to restore in the **Search and recover deleted data** section. The process of data restoration will take additional time. Click the **Next** button.
5. The program will prompt you to double-check the entered data by displaying it in the window. If all the data is correct, click the **Extract** button. The import process will start:

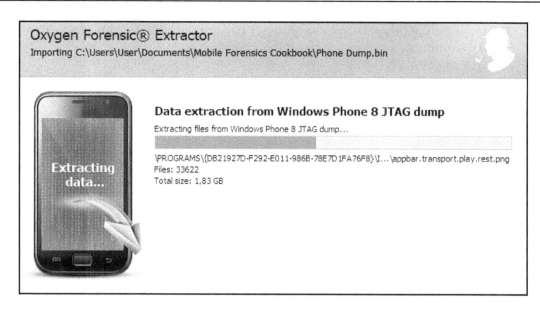

Process of physical dump analysis

6. If a file containing the encrypted screen lock password is found during the process of physical dump analysis, it will be cracked using the brute force attack:

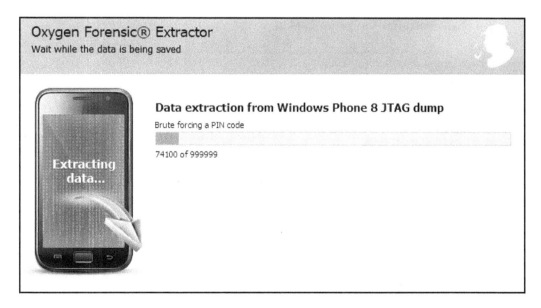

Brute forcing a PIN code

7. When the data import is finished, the final window of Oxygen Forensic Extractor with summary information about the import will be displayed.
8. Click **Open device**:

Information extracted from the Windows Phone physical dump

9. In the opened window, click on the **Device Information** section. In this section, the decrypted screen lock password will be displayed. In the previous example, this password has the value **123456**.

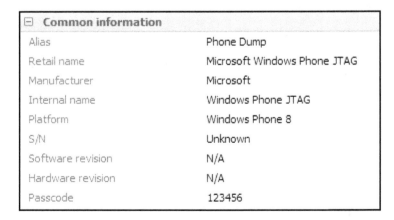

Fragment of the window of the Device Information section

Windows Phone physical dump parsing with UFED Physical Analyzer

The UFED Physical Analyzer program has already been described in Chapter 4, *Windows Phone and BlackBerry Acquisition*. In this chapter, we will describe how to extract data from a Windows Phone physical dump via UFED Physical Analyzer.

Getting ready

As was described in previous chapters, a physical dump of Windows Phone can be obtained by several methods. For example, it can be obtained via the UFED 4PC or JTAG or chip-off methods:

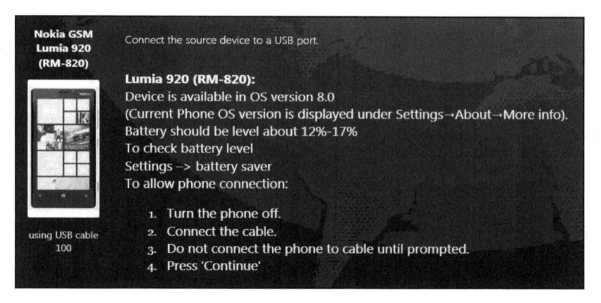

Instructions for creating a physical dump of Windows Phone using UFED 4PC

In this recipe, we will describe the analysis of Windows Phone physical dump using chip-off method.

How to do it...

1. Double-click on the icon of the UFED Physical Analyzer program. In order to import data from a Windows Phone physical dump, click **File** and **Open (advanced)** on the toolbar of the program.

2. In the opened **Open Advanced** window, click **Select Device** window. In the next window, select the model of the mobile device that corresponds to the mobile device from which the physical dump was extracted:

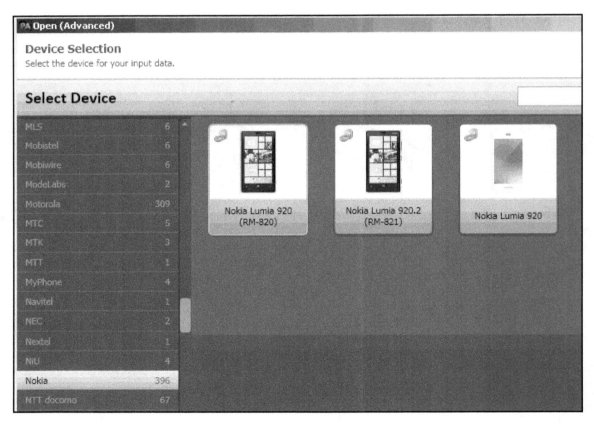

Selection of the model of mobile device in the program

3. Click the **Next** button. Ensure that the selected device has the algorithm for physical dumps analysis. Click the **Next** button:

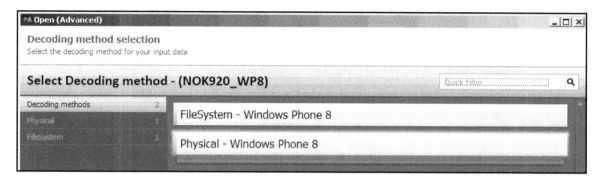

Analysis algorithms for the selected mobile device model supported by the program

4. In the next window, click the **Image** button and specify the path to the Windows Phone physical dump. Select the file and click the **Open** button:

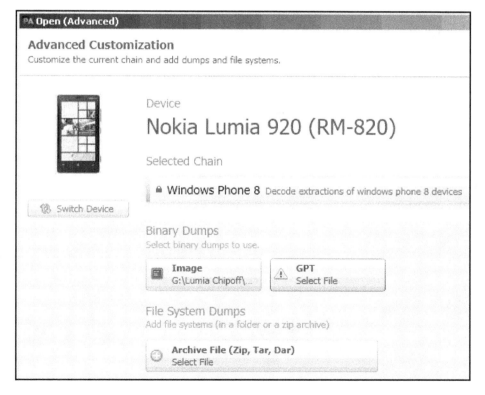

Open (Advanced) window in which the path to the physical dump of Windows Phone is specified

5. Click the **Finish** button. The extraction process will be displayed in the progress bar, which is located in the upper left corner of the program. When the extraction is finished, the categories of the extracted data will be displayed in the main window of the UFED Physical Analyzer program:

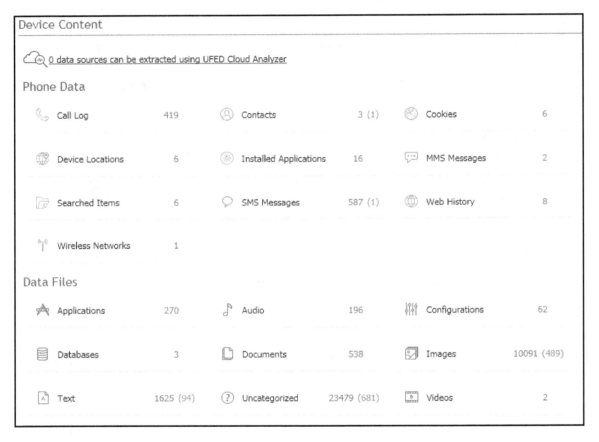

Fragment of the main window of the UFED Physical Analyzer program, which shows the categories of extracted data

11
JTAG and Chip-off Techniques

In this chapter, we'll cover the following recipes:

- A sample Android device JTAG
- A sample Android device chip-off
- A sample Windows Phone device JTAG
- A sample iPhone device chip-off

Introduction

In this chapter, we will describe methods of data extraction from mobile devices that are used only in cases when you cannot get the intended result using other methods. For example, you can use the method (chip-off) for extracting data from physical damaged devices or water damaged devices. Also, these methods are used when a mobile device is not supported by commercial mobile forensics tools or when you need to examine a damaged mobile device or even a fragment of it that has a memory chip.

These methods are:

- **JTAG** – This method is named after the name of the industry standard. Joint Test Action Group (JTAG) is a standard used for testing system boards. There is a contact pad on a system board. Using the JTAG interface, you cannot only test a system board, but you can also make a physical dump of a memory chip. This method is not destructive. The examined mobile device has to be in working order if you want to use this method.
- **Chip-off** is a destructive method, which is based on the removal of the memory chip from the system board. Then the data from the memory chip can be extracted via the programmer unit or via a special adapter. Using this method, you read information directly from the memory chip that allows examining hardly damaged mobile devices or parts of mobile devices. The use of the programmer or adapter is determined by the type of the memory chip. Although the sizes of the memory chips are standardized, there are many different form factors and due to this fact, an expert has to have a lot of different expensive adapters for this method. After removing the memory chip from the mobile device, it will be impossible to use this device.
- **ISP** is a gentle version of the chip-off method. This method does not involve memory chip desoldering from the system board of the mobile device; instead, external conductors are used to attach to it, with the help of which the data from the memory chip will be copied.

The complexity of this method is as follows:

- It is not always possible to access the contacts of the memory chip installed on the system board of the mobile device
- It is not always possible to provide high-quality contact of external conductors with contact pads of the memory chip

As a rule, the use of JTAG, chip-off, and ISP methods may require the purchase of additional expensive equipment and a highly qualified expert.

A sample Android device JTAG

Flashers are used when physical dumps of mobile devices are made with the use of the JTAG method. Flashers are devices for flashing mobile devices. Unfortunately, there is no flasher with which you could make a physical dump of any mobile device. As a rule, a flasher supports only devices of one manufacturer (Samsung, LG, Motorola, and so on) or even several models of the same manufacturer. For this reason , you have to be ready to buy or rent a flasher to make a physical dump of the examined mobile device.

There are adapters for some flashers, which are used for the connection of flashers to the system boards of mobile devices. It is recommended to purchase such adapters, as they reduce the time spent on the connection of the flasher to the mobile device. Moreover, in modern mobile devices, the density of JTAG contacts is so high that there is no other option but to connect a flasher to a system board via an adapter.

Flashers can save the extracted data in their own format. You may need additional software for extracted data conversion into another format, which will be suitable for analysis via mobile forensics tools.

The most well-known flashers in mobile forensics are: RIFF BOX, Medusa BOX, and Z3X EasyJTAG BOX.

In addition to the data extraction, flashers can help to unlock bootloaders in some Android mobile devices. A bootloader is a piece of software that is executed every time the hardware device is powered up. A bootloader may be locked. Nobody can change it. A bootloader may be unlocked. Somebody can change it. The locked bootloader is an obstacle to the super user's rights . When you have super user's rights you can easily make a physical dump of a mobile device via tools described in previous chapters.

There are mobile devices that do not have JTAG contact pads on their system boards, meaning that it is impossible to extract data using the JTAG method from such devices.

As flashers are not forensic equipment, you have to be very attentive and careful when you use them. Otherwise, you can damage or destroy the data contained on the mobile device.

The fact that encryption of userdata partition is used more often in modern mobile devices makes this method of data extraction from the mobile device inapplicable. In this recipe, we will describe the sample of data extraction from the Samsung GT-I9192 smartphone via Z3X EasyJTAG BOX.

How to do it...

1. Disassemble the smartphone and extract the system board before the data extraction.
2. Double click the icon of the control program of the Z3X EasyJTAG BOX - Z3X EasyJtag BOX JTAG Classic Suite. In the opened window of the program, select the model of the mobile device - Samsung GT-I9192. In the main window, there will be displayed the interface circuit of the smartphone and the flasher:

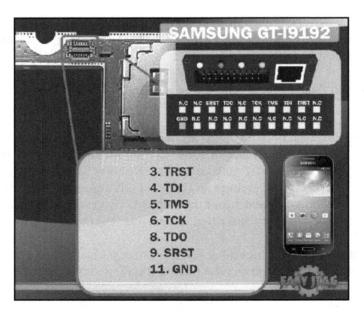

The interface circuit of Z3X EasyJTAG BOX and Samsung GT-I9192

3. Using short copper wires, connect the Z3X EasyJTAG BOX with the Samsung GT-I9192.

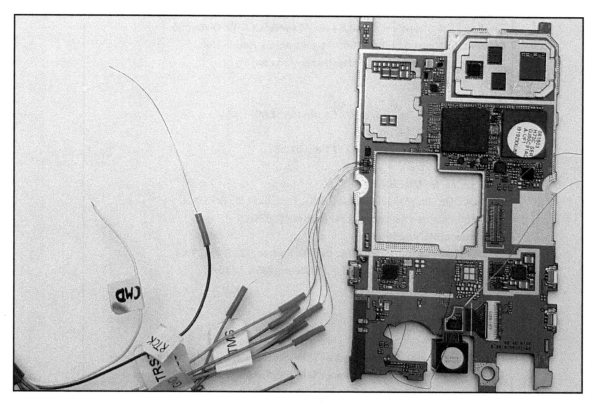

The connection of Z3X EasyJTAG BOX with Samsung GT-I9192

4. Turn on the flasher. After that, the information about the connected device will be displayed in the **Z3X EasyJtag BOX JTAG Classic Suite** program window:

```
EasyJtag Suite Classic ver.: 2.5.0.8 / wxWidgets 3.1.0-W-U started.
OS ver.: Windows 8 (build 9200), 64-bit edition. Admin righ
For support and updates visit http://easy-jtag.com
Check security...
OK
Initialising: SAMSUNG GT-I9192 Config ver.:1.00
I/O Level set to : 2200 mV
Box S/N: 0700300615225362 ,FW Ver.: 01.58
Connecting to Target...
JTAG device: MSM8230AB.
CPU IDCODE : 0x4F1F0F0F Mfg.: 0x787, Part: 0xf1f0, Ver.: 0x4
CPU Manufacturer: Samsung , CPU Name: ARM7GEN
JTAG device: MSM8230AB.
CPU IDCODE : 0x308A30E1 Mfg.: 0x070, Part: 0x08a3, Ver.: 0x3
CPU Manufacturer: QUALCOMM , CPU Name: MSM8230AB
Halting CPU...
Initialize hardware...
Starting target communication...
Detecting emmc memory parameters of bank (0) ...
EMMC #0 : ID : 0x00000045 Name : SEM08G Size : 7,3 G , (15269888) Blocks
EMMC #1 : ID : 0x00000045 Name : SEM08G Size : 2,0 M , (4096) Blocks
eMMC flash device(s) found, Device ID : 0x00450000
```

Information about connected device

5. Verify that the device's memory size is displayed correctly (8 GB) and the start address of the memory reads **Start (HEX)** and the size of the memory fragment **Length (HEX)** is correctly set. If necessary, specify the name of the file to which the data will be read. Click the **Read eMMC Card** button.

6. When the extraction is complete, you will receive a file with the `.bin` extension containing a copy of the mobile device's memory.

7. The structure of this file corresponds to the structure of the physical dump obtained from a similar device via mobile forensics tools. To verify that the mobile device's memory dump was made correctly, use the free AccessData FTK Imager tool. Download the tool from the developer's website and double click the installation file. Install the program following the instructions. When the program is installed, double click its icon. When the program is started, select **File** | **Add Evidence Item...** in its toolbar. In the opened **Select Source** window, tick **Image File** and click the **Next** button. In the next window, click **Browse...** and select the created flasher bin-file. Click the **Finish** button.

8. After that, you will be able to view partitions, folders, and files that are contained in the memory of the mobile device:

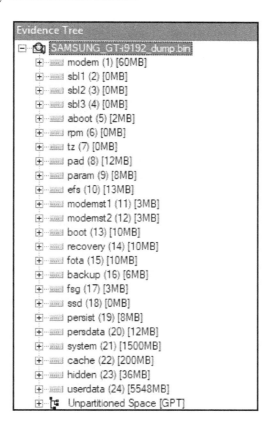

Partitions of the Samsung GT-I9192 mobile device

The user's data is contained in the **userdata** partition.

See also

- The website of the Z3X EasyJTAG BOX producer: http://easy-jtag.com/
- The website of the FTK Imager program: http://accessdata.com/

A sample Android device chip-off

For some of our colleagues, the data extraction from a device damaged by fire or water, or even from a piece of a system board seems to be a miracle. However, it is routine for us.

Most of the memory chips that are used in mobile devices have eMMC (embedded MMC) types. These chips are used when the memory chips are soldered to the system boards of devices. These memory chips have the same interface as SD cards. That is why you can read the information from this kind of memory card just by soldering the memory card pinouts to the pinouts of your card reader. However, it is more convenient to do it using specialized adapters. As memory chips have different sizes, companies specializing in the distribution of equipment for data extraction from eMMC chips sell such adapters in sets. For example, you can buy a set of adapters with the SMARTPHONE KIT from the Rusolut company, the use of which will almost guarantee that you will be able to read information from any memory chip. Also, a similar set of adapters is included in the PC-3000 MOBILE set of the ACE lab company. You can buy adapters separately or sets of adapters from the Allsocket company.

On Aliexpress or on eBay, you can buy adapters separately or sets of adapters for the eMMS readings of other manufacturers.

In the popular smartphone models, UFS chips for data storage are increasingly used. UP828 Programmer with the adapter is used for data extraction from such chips.

Getting ready

Disassemble the phone and remove the system board. As a rule, chips on the system boards are covered with metal cases, which you need to remove. When the metal cases are removed, use markings on the chips to understand which one is the memory chip. The memory chip is always located next to a microprocessor:

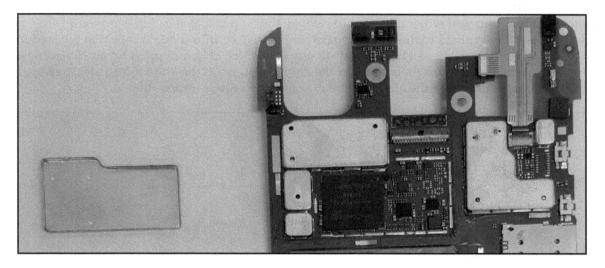

Memory chip that was covered with the metal case on the system board of the mobile device

How to do it...

You need to remove the memory chip from the system board. The chip must be heated in a certain sequence, avoiding overheating. The heating temperature should be sufficient to melt the solder, with which the chip is soldered to the system board. If the solder is not melted, you will damage the chip during the process of removing it. If you overheat the chip, the data on the chip will be lost. You need to use a soldering station with a wide nozzle and temperature sensor, which has to be placed on the chip to control its temperature. You can find heating modes for particular chips on the internet.

If you cannot find the heating mode to your chip, we recommend the following: heat the chip for 2 minutes at the temperature of 100 degrees Celsius. Then heat the chip for 5 minutes at the temperature of 230 degrees Celsius. Hold the nozzle of the soldering station as close to the chip as possible. This is important, because when the distance between the nozzle and the chip increases, the temperature of hot air drops rapidly. It is important not to miss the moment when the small components located next to the memory chip on the system board will begin to shift. This indicates that the solder under the memory chip has melted. However, you will not be able to remove the chip yet, as the chip is not only soldered, but also glued to the system board with epoxy resin. When you see that the solder has melted, put the back of a utility knife to any side of the chip and press firmly, inserting the blade between the system board and the chip. If you press the knife too hard it may lead to mechanical damage of the chip and the examination will be impossible:

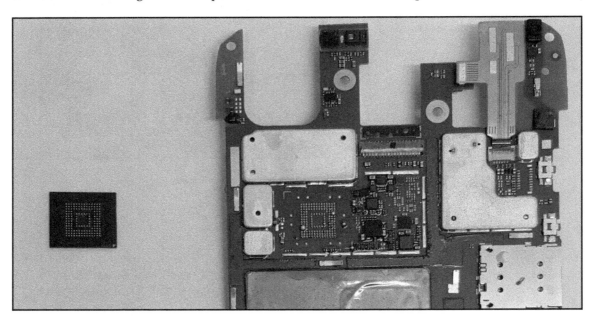

The memory chip removed from the system board

When the memory chip is removed from the system board, you need to clean it from the remains of epoxy resin and cover the contacts with the layer of solder. There should not be any problems with the contacts being covered with a new layer of solder, but the cleaning from epoxy resin can be difficult. There are two main methods of cleaning chips from epoxy resin:

- **Method 1: chemical:** Removal of epoxy resin is done with the help of special mixtures.
- **Method 2: mechanical:** The chip is heated with the hot air from the soldering station. The epoxy resin becomes soft and it is scraped off mechanically. This procedure causes a strong smell and for that reason, you need to do it in a well-ventilated place or in a ventilation hood.

When the memory chip is ready for the examination, place it on the adapter and connect to your computer:

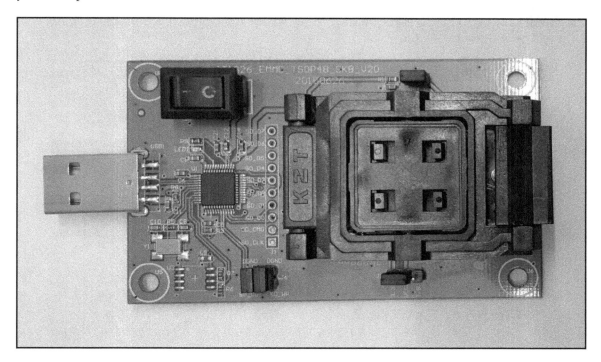

Adapter for data reading from the memory chip

As such adapters are not specialized forensic equipment, their use does not exclude the recording of information on the connected memory chip. For that reason, you must use a software write blocker (for example, SAFE Block) or a hardware write blocker (for example, Tableau UltraBlock USB3 (T8u)).

To create a forensic image of the memory chip, you can use any forensic software that has this functionality. For example, AccessData FTK Imager, which has been described already in this chapter. Double click the icon of the program. When the program is started, go to the toolbar and click **File | Create Disk Image….** In the next window, in the list, select the drive that corresponds to the memory chip. Click the **Finish** button.

In the **Create Image** window, click the **Add** button. In the **Select Image Type** window, check the **Raw (dd)** box, and click the **Next** button. In the **Evidence Item Information** window, you can add a description of your case. Click the **Next** button. In the **Select Image Destination** window, click the **Browse** button and specify the path to save the data. In the **Image Filename (Excluding Extension)** field, specify the filename. In the **Image Fragment Size (MB)** field, set the value to zero. All the data extracted from the memory chip will be written to one file:

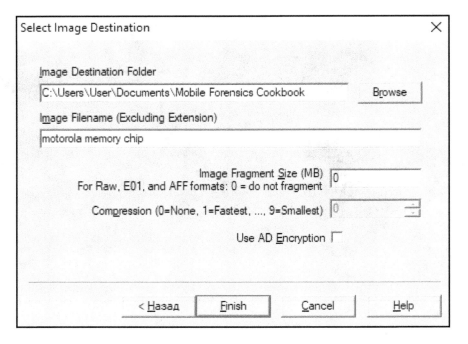

The appearance of the Select Image Destination window

Click the **Finish** button. Click the **Start** button. The process of creating forensic copy of the data contained in the memory chip will start.

At the end of this process, the image can be analyzed via mobile forensic software. Double-click on the Autopsy icon and follow the steps for the physical dump analysis of the Android mobile device that was described in `Chapter 8`, *Analyzing Physical Dumps and Backups of Android Devices*. The next figure shows the results of the analysis:

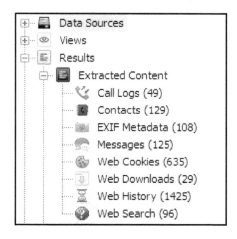

The results of the memory chip dump analysis

There's more...

- The article, *Extracting data from damaged mobile devices*: `https://articles.forensicfocus.com/2013/08/21/extracting-data-from-damaged-mobile-devices/`
- The article, *Chip-off technique in mobile forensics*: `https://www.digitalforensics.com/blog/chip-off-technique-in-mobile-forensics/`

See also

- The website of the Rusolut company: `https://rusolut.com/`
- PC-3000 MOBILE: Unique all-in-one solution for recovering data from mobile devices: `http://www.acelaboratory.com/news/newsitem.php?itemid=206`
- The website of the Allsocket company: `http://allsocket.com/`

- The website of UP828 Programmer: `http://www.vipprogrammer.com/`
- The website of SAFE Block: `https://www.forensicsoft.com/`

A sample Windows Phone device JTAG

Using JTAG and chip-off methods is, in fact, the only way to get the physical dumps from Windows Phone mobile devices. Also, these methods are used to extract data from screen-locked mobile devices. In this recipe, we will describe a sample of data extraction from Nokia Lumia 925 (RM-892) using the JTAG method.

How to do it...

1. Before data extraction, disassemble the smartphone and get the access to it system board:

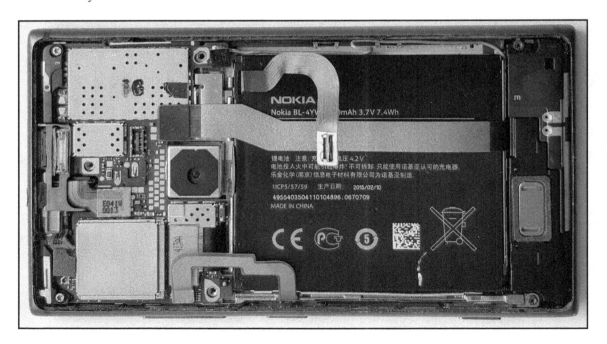

System board of Nokia Lumia 925

2. Double-click on the Z3X EasyJTAG BOX control program icon - **Z3X EasyJtag BOX JTAG Classic Suite**. In the opened window, select the model of the mobile device - Nokia Lumia 925. The interface circuit of the device with the flasher will be displayed in the main window of the program:

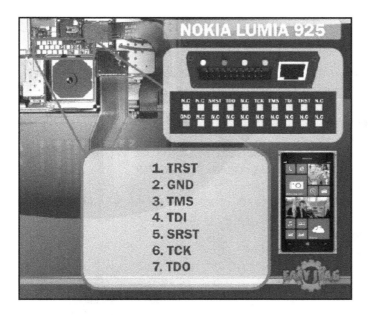

The interface circuit of Z3X EasyJTAG BOX and Nokia Lumia 925

3. Using short copper wires, connect the Z3X EasyJTAG BOX with Nokia Lumia 925:

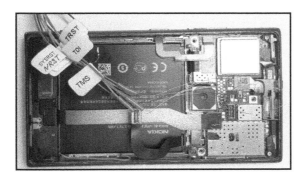

Connection of Z3X EasyJTAG BOX with Nokia Lumia 925

4. Switch on the flasher. In the main window of the **Z3X EasyJtag BOX JTAG Classic Suite**, the information about the connected device will be displayed:

```
EasyJtag Suite Classic ver.: 2.5.0.8 / wxWidgets 3.1.0-W-U started.
OS ver.: Windows 8 (build 9200), 64-bit edition. Admin righ
For support and updates visit http://easy-jtag.com
Check security...
OK
Initialising: NOKIA LUMIA 925 Config ver.:1.00
I/O Level set to : 2200 mV
Box S/N: 0700300615225362 ,FW Ver.: 01.58
Connecting to Target...
JTAG device: MSM8960.
CPU IDCODE : 0x4F1F0F0F Mfg.: 0x787, Part: 0xf1f0, Ver.: 0x4
CPU Manufacturer: Samsung , CPU Name: ARM7GEN
JTAG device: MSM8960.
CPU IDCODE : 0x706B40E1 Mfg.: 0x070, Part: 0x06b4, Ver.: 0x7
CPU Manufacturer: QUALCOMM , CPU Name: MSM8960 Rev 0.8
Halting CPU...
Initialize hardware...
Starting target communication...
Detecting emmc memory parameters of bank (0) ...
EMMC #0 : ID : 0x00000015 Name : MAG2WA Size : 14,6 G , (30535680) Blocks
EMMC #1 : ID : 0x00000015 Name : MAG2WA Size : 2,0 M , (4096) Blocks
eMMC flash device(s) found, Device ID : 0x00150000
```

Information about the connected device

5. Verify that the device's memory size is displayed correctly (8 GB) and the start address of the memory reads **Start (HEX)** and the size of the memory fragment **Length (HEX)**, is correctly set. If necessary, specify the name of the file to which the data will be read. Click the **Read eMMC Card** button.

6. When the extraction is complete, you will receive a file with the `.bin` extension containing a copy of the mobile device's memory.

7. In order to process the extracted data, let's use Oxygen Forensic. Double-click on the icon of the program.

8. To import data from this JTAG image, click the arrow to the right of the **Import File** button on the Oxygen Forensic toolbar. In the drop-down menu, go to **Import Android backup / image** and then **Import Windows Phone JTAG Image:**

Selection of the type of data import

9. In the opened window, specify the path to the JTAG image. Select it and click **Open**.

10. In the new window, fill in the details of the case, such as: **Device alias, Case number, Evidence number, Place, Incident number, Inspector, Device owner, Owner email,** and so on. If necessary, select the data that you want to restore in the **Search and recover deleted data** section. The data restoring will take additional time. Click the **Next** button. The program will prompt you to double-check the entered data by displaying it in the window. If all the data is correct, click the **Extract** button. The import process will start.

11. When the process of data importing is finished, the final window of Oxygen Forensic Extractor with summary information about the import will be displayed. Click the **Finish** button to finish the data extraction. The extracted data will be available for viewing and analysis:

Information extracted from Windows Phone JTAG memory dump

A sample iPhone device chip-off

We all know the importance of physical dumps of mobile devices. Only the physical dumps allow an expert to retrieve the maximum of data from the examined device. The physical dump extraction becomes a pressing issue, when we need to examine a screen locked device or damaged device. Unfortunately, the physical dump extraction from Apple mobile devices is a huge problem. At conferences among colleagues, there are rumors that someone was able to extract data from an iPhone using the chip-off technique. This is the truth and a lie at the same time. The thing is that starting from iPhone 3GS, Apple mobile devices are encrypted, meaning that the use of the chip-off method does not make any sense. Some experts suggest to use the brute force method to decrypt physical dumps of Apple devices. However, if you are familiar with the Apple iOS Security document, you will understand that it is meaningless to decrypt these dumps using the brute force method. The chip-off method can be used in the early models of Apple mobile devices, where there is no encryption.

In this recipe, we will describe the data extraction from iPhone 3G. There is no encryption of user data in this device.

Getting ready

Remove the system board from the device. There is only one memory chip in the DIP package in such devices. It will be easy to find it.

How to do it...

1. Use the soldering station, heat the chip for 2 minutes at the temperature of 100 degrees Celsius. Then heat the chip for 5 minutes at the temperature of 230 degrees Celsius. Hold the nozzle of the soldering station as close to the chip as possible; it is important, because when the distance between the nozzle and the chip increases, the temperature of hot air drops rapidly. If you did everything correctly, the chip should be easily removed from the system board:

The memory chip removed from the system board of iPhone 3G

2. As the chip has a standard DIP package, create its image using any programmer unit designed to work with such chips. Place the chip on the programmer unit's pad and read the data from the chip to the file via the control program of the programming tool.

3. The next important step is the preliminary processing of the extracted data and bringing it to a state when it can be processed by mobile forensics tools.

4. The difficulty is that in addition to the data sectors, technical headers are extracted from the chip, which contain additional information. These headers interfere with the analysis of the dump via mobile forensics tools. Also, the entire memory area of the chip is divided into segments that are interconnected as RAID. However, it is not a big problem. The ACE Lab company has a solution base, where it describes how to properly configure the extracted data so it is available for further analysis:

Controller marking	Number of memory chips	Number of parts	Memory chip marking	Memory chip ID	Capacity(Mb)
iPhone 3G 8GB	1	2	MT29F32G08TAA	0x2CD7D53E	8192
iPhone 3G 8Gb	1	4	TC58NVG4D1DTG00	0x98D594BA	8192
iPhone 3G A1241	1	4	K9LBG08U0M	0xECD755B6	16384
iPhone SA S5L8900X	1	4	K9WAG08U0M	0xECD551A6	8192
iPhone SA ARM_S5L8900X	1	2	JS29F32G08FAMC1	0x89D7D53E	8192

Fragment of solutions from the ACE Lab knowledge base

5. Use the control program of the programmer PC 3000 FLASH and a solution from their knowledge base that will allow you to configure the data extracted from the chip in the right way. If you did everything correctly, then in the program you will see information about the filesystem of the mobile device:

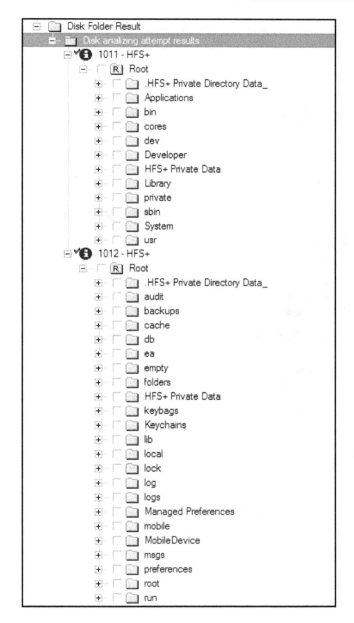

The result of extracted data configuration

6. Save the result in the new file. Now the file is available for the analysis via mobile forensics tools.

7. Double click the UFED Physical Analyzer icon. In the toolbar, click **File | Open (advanced)**. In the **Open (Advanced)** window, click the **Select Device** button:

Selection of extraction type

8. Select the device **Apple iPhone (Physical)**. Click the **Next** button. Click the **Next** button again. In the next window, click the **Image** button and specify the location of your file. Click the **Open** button. Click the **Finish** button. The process of the analysis of data extracted from the iPhone will start. At the end of the analysis, its results will be displayed in the program window:

Device Content

 0 data sources can be extracted using UFED Cloud Analyzer

Phone Data

Data Files

	Configurations	624		Databases	501		Images	1309
?	Uncategorized	1282		Videos	6			

The results of data analysis extracted from iPhone 3G

Refer to the article, *Extracting data from a damaged iPhone via chip-off technique*: `https://www.digitalforensics.com/blog/extracting-data-from-a-damaged-iphone-via-chip-off-technique/`.
Refer to the article, *Extracting data from a damaged iPhone via chip-off technique part 2*: `https://www.digitalforensics.com/blog/extracting-data-from-a-damaged-iphone-via-chip-off-technique-part-2/`
Ace Lab Solution Centre: `http://www.pc-3000flash.com/solbase/task.php?group_id=321lang=eng`

See also

- iOS Security: `https://www.apple.com/business/docs/iOS_Security_Guide.pdf`

- PC 3000 Flash: `http://www.acelaboratory.com/pc3000flash.php`
- iPhone 6 data recovery from a dead logic board: `https://www.youtube.com/watch?v=58-7cg9cYNY`

Index

www.ingramcontent.com/pod-product-compliance
Lightning Source LLC
Chambersburg PA
CBHW080627060326
40690CB00021B/4845